S0-DFI-192

BOOMER HUMOR

Jokes About Baby Boomers Growing Old Ungracefully

SPECIAL LARGE PRINT
EDITION

Glen Warner

FOLK
LORE
PUBLISHING

© 2011 by Folklore Publishing
First printed in 2011 10 9 8 7 6 5 4 3 2 1
Printed in Canada

All rights reserved. No part of this work covered by the copyrights hereon may be reproduced or used in any form or by any means—graphic, electronic or mechanical—without the prior written permission of the publisher, except for reviewers, who may quote brief passages. Any request for photocopying, recording, taping or storage on information retrieval systems of any part of this work shall be directed in writing to the publisher.

The Publisher: Folklore Publishing
Website: www.folklorepublishing.com

Library and Archives Canada Cataloguing in Publication

Warner, Glen, 1947–
   Boomer humor : jokes about baby boomers growing
old ungracefully / Glen Warner.

Issued also in electronic format.
ISBN 978-1-926677-76-7

   1. Aging—Humor. 2. Older people—Humor. 3. Baby boom generation—Humor. I. Title.

PN6231.A43W37 2011   C818'.602 C2011-902474-8

Project Director: Faye Boer
Project Editor: Kathy van Denderen
Cover Image: © 2011 iStockphoto/Brett Lamb

We acknowledge the support of the Alberta Foundation for the Arts for our publishing program.

We acknowledge the financial support of the Government of Canada through the Canada Book Fund (CBF) for our publishing activities.

PC: 5

❧ Contents ❧

A Note from the Author 6

CHAPTER 1:
Boomer Humor? Get Used to It, Baby! 9

CHAPTER 2:
Nostalgia Isn't What It Used To Be 13

CHAPTER 3:
Defying Gravity 31

CHAPTER 4:
The Viagra Monologues 42

CHAPTER 5:
Little Romances 57

CHAPTER 6:
Until Death Do Us Part 75

CHAPTER 7:
Family Matters 117

CHAPTER 8:
Driving Disasters 133

CHAPTER 9:
Diseases and Losses 143

CHAPTER 10:
Assorted Eccentricities 169

CHAPTER 11:
Going Ga-ga 183

CHAPTER 12:
Last Laughs 207

Dedication

For Diane,
still laughing after all these years

Acknowledgments

I would like to thank my publisher, Faye Boer,
for sticking her neck way out once again
and publishing another collection of my jokes.
I must also thank my editor,
Kathy van Denderen, who drew the short
straw and got lumbered with this project.

Much love and special thanks must also
be extended to my multi-talented wife, Diane,
for keeping my ancient computer working so
I could finish this book on time, and for laughing
at my jokes over the 40-odd and often crazy years
I've spent accumulating them.

❧✕❧

A Note from the Author

If you're a Baby Boomer like me, you're probably getting used to people around you making fun of your advancing years. Once we enter our 50s, it seems that friends and family think nothing of calling us names like "old fart," geezer" or something much worse, just because we occasionally commit some minor social faux pas or another.

I mean, what's the big deal if we momentarily forget our spouse's name from time to time? What does that prove? And so what if we get confused once in a while and put our car in "drive" instead of "reverse" and crash into a store window or two. Hell, that could happen to anybody. And wouldn't you love to know what young people find so funny about a Boomer-aged man or woman who sometimes has trouble making it to the toilet on time?

Mind you, if you're 50 or so and completely honest with yourself, I'll bet you've already recognized a few of the signs of becoming a chronologically challenged Baby Boomer, such as when you first notice that you now have more strands of hair in your ears than you do on your head. Or when you first observe that you often blackout whenever you stand up too quickly. Or when you first come to terms with the new reality that from now on you must never, *ever* take a sleeping pill and a laxative on the same night.

For some people, the slide into aging Boomerdom has nothing to do with physical ailments at all. It's about entering a strange state of mind that compels them to do odd things. Like spending hours sorting old screws and nails into little jars. Or driving across town to save

10 cents on a carton of milk. Or discovering one day that they're scared out of their wits to drive at the speed limit.

For others, it's becoming nostalgic about their youth. They start to bore their children and grandchildren with long-winded stories that begin, "In my day, we..." Or they drag out old photographs and take pride in showing everyone where their hairline was back when The Beatles were screaming "I Wanna Hold Your Hand."

For me, it was simply a matter of looking in the mirror one day and realizing that after years of writing jokes that poke fun at old geezers, I had become one myself.

It occurred to me that millions of other Baby Boomers like me are probably coming to terms with the same reality—we're all on the cusp of that great long slide into feeblemindedness, and there isn't a damn thing we can do about it except laugh our way through our predicament.

Boomer Humor is a compilation of jokes that celebrate the plight of millions of Baby Boomers who suddenly find themselves growing old ungracefully. All the stuff you'd expect is here—jokes about plastic surgery gone wrong, bizarre driving mishaps, arthritis, menopause, Alzheimer's and dementia. There are also jokes and riddles about flagging libidos, the joy of sex in advancing years, horny grannies chasing reluctant grandpas, and, of course, lots and lots of jokes about Viagra.

No book about the darker side of the aging process would be complete without some good old-fashioned toilet humor, so I've also included a lot of jokes about constipation, incontinence, Boomers who suffer with dreadful gastric-release issues and the funnier aspects of depending on Depends. As well, sprinkled among the jokes are humorous quotes about aging and living life to the fullest in senior years from some famous older folks such as George Burns, Woody Allen, Groucho Marx, George Carlin and Willie Nelson, among others.

As you'll see, aging can be funny as hell. We all seem to have a deep-seated need to laugh at ourselves, and what could be funnier than watching fellow Boomers—that generation of people who once believed they'd never get old—all starting to fall apart and go ga-ga?

As I see it, life is like a roll of toilet paper—the closer it gets to the end, the faster it goes. The only sensible thing we Boomers can do now is laugh our way into our dotage. Look at it this way: it's better to be an old fart than a young upstart, it's more fun to be a schleppy than a preppy, and it's much better to be a clever old smartass than a stupid young dumbass.

So sit back, relax, take your medication, pour yourself a stiff one and enjoy these jokes. If you find any of them laugh-out-loud funny (dare I say pee-your-pants funny?), you probably are an aging Boomer whether you're willing to admit it or not.

Take comfort in the knowledge that getting older is just a matter of perspective. After all, we've been told for years that it's just a state of mind, right? If it's true, as the saying goes, that you're only as old as you feel, then I keep asking myself, how can I still be alive at 150?

Have fun!

Glen Warner

CHAPTER ONE

Boomer Humor? Get Used to It, Baby!

You know you're an aging baby Boomer when...

- you need to change your underwear after every sneeze
- "getting a little action" means you don't need to take a laxative
- you tell your doctor you think you've got "fluid on the knee," and he says you're just not aiming straight
- you talk about "good grass," and you're referring to your lawn
- performance anxiety now refers to your golf score
- "twice a night" now refers to bathroom visits

> "Age is mind over matter. If you don't mind, it doesn't matter."
>
> –Mark Twain

- you notice that without your visits to your cardiologist, your dermatologist, your urologist, your denturist and your proctologist, you'd have no social life at all
- your optometrist tells you that the "UFOs" you keep seeing are just "spots before your eyes"
- you're cautioned to "slow down" by your doctor, instead of the police
- "getting lucky" means finding your car in a parking lot

- you wake up with "that morning after feeling" when you didn't do anything the night before
- you still think you're the life of the party, so long as it doesn't go on past 8:00 PM
- your idea of "happy hour" is nap time
- you sit in a rocking chair and can't get it going
- your knees buckle and your belt won't
- you get winded playing chess
- you've reached the age when you stop lying about your age and start bragging about it
- your children look middle-aged
- you have too much room in your house, but not enough in your medicine cabinet
- the little gray-haired lady you help across the street is your wife
- you throw a party and your neighbors aren't even aware of it
- you are proud of your lawnmower
- your knees are more accurate at predicting changes in the weather than the meteorologists on The Weather Channel
- you observe that now your dreams are dry and your farts are wet
- you notice that half the items in your shopping cart say "For Fast Relief"
- you find that when visiting family, you can't go more than two hours without popping some aspirin, a tranquilizer or a Beano

- the word "toothbrush" suddenly takes on a literal meaning
- magazine articles with titles like "Test Yourself for Alzheimer's" or "How to Survive a Nursing Home Fire" suddenly catch your eye
- friends compliment you on your new alligator shoes—and you're barefoot
- instead of renting *Debbie Does Dallas* from the porno video store, you now borrow *Debbie Does Dialysis* from your local library

> "Old age isn't so bad when you consider the alternative."
>
> –Maurice Chevalier

- a road sign announcing "No Services for the Next 25 Miles" sends your bladder into a panic
- you begin reading obituaries obsessively, paying special attention to how long each deceased person lived
- you start believing that laugh lines make you look distinguished
- you choose hats solely by their SPF factor
- the term "alternative medicine" now just means taking either Gravol or Maalox
- you spend a lot of time thinking about hell and the hereafter—like when you walk into a room and say to yourself, "What the hell am I here after?"
- your main forms of exercise are now Bingo, checkers and flossing after dinner
- your idea of weight lifting is standing up

- you enjoy hearing about other people's operations
- your bathroom cabinet contains Prozac, Polident and Grecian Formula and Depends
- you always keep a ready stash of suppositories, a blood pressure kit and a defibrillator on hand
- to you, "CD" means "Certificate of Deposit"
- you go for a mammogram and realize that from now on this is probably the only time someone will ask you to appear topless on film
- you now get the same sensation from a rocking chair that you once got from a roller coaster
- you realize that the only "wild oats" you have left are in your breakfast cereal
- you can no longer open childproof caps—without the aid of a hammer
- you notice that now, when you go braless, your boobs pull all the wrinkles out of your face
- an "all nighter" means not needing to get up to pee
- others worry that you are dead when you fall asleep
- you notice that the more you complain, the longer God lets you live
- you realize one day that the next diaper you change will probably be your own

CHAPTER TWO

Nostalgia Isn't What It Used To Be

The year is 1960 and a hip young guy named Billy Bob hops into his '56 Chevy and heads out to pick up his date, Peggy Sue. Her father answers the door and invites Billy Bob in and asks him to take a seat in the living room while his daughter gets ready.

"So what have you kids got planned for tonight?" asks the father.

"Well, sir," says Billy Bob, "I think we'll go for a malt and then when it gets dark we'll probably head over to the drive-in to see a movie."

"Why don't you kids go out and screw?" asks the father. "I hear all the kids are doing it."

"Huh?" says Billy Bob, his eyes lighting up.

"Yeah," says the father. "Peggy Sue loves to screw. Why, she'd stay out all night screwing if we let her."

"Really?" says Billy Bob, who is smiling from ear to ear as he mentally revises his plans for the evening.

Then Peggy Sue comes bouncing down the stairs wearing a tight sweater, a short pleated skirt and knee socks. "Are you ready?" she says to Billy Bob.

"You kids have a fun evening," says Peggy Sue's dad as the teenagers eagerly run down the steps to Billy Bob's car.

An hour later, Peggy Sue bursts in the front door of her home, her hair disheveled and her clothes all askew and torn.

"Goddammit, Dad," she screams, "how many times do I have to tell you, it's called The Twist. The Twist!"

Q: How many '60s folk musicians does it take to change a light bulb?

A: Ten. One to change the bulb and nine others to moan about it.

Little Ernest is looking through the family photo album with his mother. He spots a photograph of a skinny young guy with shoulder-length hair, a guitar under one arm and his other arm wrapped around the boy's mother. "Who's the weird guy in this picture with you?" he asks.

His mother smiles at the picture, which rekindles fond memories. "That's your father," she says, laughing.

> "You know you're getting old when you stop to tie your shoelaces and wonder what else you could do when you're down there."
>
> –George Burns

"Oh, yeah?" says Ernest. "Well, then who's the paunchy old bald guy we're living with now?"

Then And Now

1965	2011
acid rock	acid reflux
all you need is love	all you need is All-Bran
cool	drool
feelin' groovy	feeling woozy
going out to a new, hip joint	getting a new hip joint
growing pot	growing a pot belly
long hair	longing for hair
moving to California because it's cool	moving to California because it's hot
passing your driver's test	passing your vision test
peace and love	peace and quiet
perfect high	perfect high-yield mutual fund
Rolling Stones	kidney stones
screw the system	upgrade the system
sex, drugs and rock and roll	Ex-Lax, prescription drugs and on the dole
taking acid	taking antacid
trying to act like Keith Richards	trying not to act like Keith Richards
The Times They Are A-Changin'	time to see if your Depends need changing

OH, TO BE YOUNG AND DATING AGAIN
PART I

- When you're young and dating, your handsome new beau takes you out for a good time.

  When you're an aging Boomer, your old man brings home a six-pack for himself and says, "So what are you going to drink tonight?"

- When you're young and dating, your dude hugs you tenderly for no reason.

  When you're an aging Boomer, your drunken hubby grabs your boobs and squeezes them while making an annoying honking noise.

- When you're young and dating, farting is never an issue.

  When you're an aging Boomer, you make sure the old gas bag is never sitting next to an open flame.

- When you're young and dating, you enjoy foreplay.

  When you're an aging Boomer, you say, "If we have sex, will you leave me alone?"

- When you're young and dating, a single bed for two feels cozy.

  When you're an aging Boomer, your king-size bed feels kinda cramped.

- When you're young and dating, the sight of him naked turns you on.

  When you're an aging Boomer, you look at him and say to yourself, "Was he always that fat?"

- When you're young and dating, you picture the two of you growing old together.

  When you're an aging Boomer, you look at him and wonder, "Who will die first?"

It's 1965 and little Billy is visiting his grand-mother one afternoon. He asks her, "How come you don't have a boyfriend, Grandma, now that Grandpa has gone to heaven?"

"My television is my boyfriend," replies the grandmother. "I sit here in my bedroom and watch it all day. The religious programs make me feel good, and the comedies make me laugh. I'm quite happy with my TV as my boyfriend."

Just then the picture on the grandmother's old black-and-white TV goes snowy, and she begins to fiddle with the knobs on front and tries to adjust the rabbit ears on top to try to get the signal back. When nothing works, she hits the top and sides of the TV with the palm of her hand.

Then the doorbell rings and little Billy runs to answer it. A woman from next door is on the porch. "Is your grandmother home?" she asks.

"Yeah, she is," replies Billy. "But she can't speak to you now because she's in the bedroom banging her boyfriend."

Two Boomer-aged guys, Wilbur and Luke, are talking about modern values. "In my day, I didn't sleep with my wife before we got married," says Wilbur. "Did you?"

"I'm not sure," replies Luke. "What was her maiden name?"

OH, TO BE YOUNG AND DATING AGAIN
PART II

- When you're young and dating, he says, "You take my breath away."

  When you're an aging Boomer, you say, "You make me feel like I'm suffocating."

- When you're young and dating, you have sex two times a week.

  When you're an aging Boomer, you have sex two times a year.

- When you're young and dating, you love the way he takes control of things.

  When you're an aging Boomer, you think, "He's nothing but a control freak."

- When you're young and dating, he makes you feel like a million dollars.

  When you're an aging Boomer, you think, "If I had a dime for every stupid thing he's said or done..."

- When you're young and dating, you say, "Don't stop!"

  When you're an aging Boomer, you say, "Don't start!"

- When you're young and dating, he says, "Is that all you're eating?"

  When you're an aging Boomer, he says, "Maybe you should just have a salad, dear."

- When you're young and dating, he's turbo-charged.

  When you're an aging Boomer, he needs a jumpstart.

- When you're young and dating, he shops at Victoria's Secret.

  When you're an aging Boomer, he shops at Fruit of the Loom.

- When you're young and dating, it's feathers and handcuffs.

  When you're an aging Boomer, it's ball and chain.

- When you're young and dating, you say, "When we are together, time stands still."

  When you're an aging Boomer, you say, "This goddamned relationship is going nowhere."

- When you're young and dating, it's oysters and champagne.

  When you're an aging Boomer, it's fish sticks and beer.

- When you're young and dating, you say, "I can't believe we found each other."

  When you're an aging Boomer, you say to yourself, "How did I end up with this asshole?"

Q: How do you know if an old country singer is on Prozac?

A: He buys back his house, his wife forgives him and his dog comes back to life.

Three Boomer guys are having coffee and reminiscing about their lives. One guy says, "I can remember being pushed around in my stroller. I must have been only two or three years old."

Another guy says, "Oh, yeah? Well, I can remember standing up in my crib for the very first time."

The third guy says, "That's nothing. I can remember going to a picnic with my father and going home with my mother."

HOW WE VIEW SUCCESS IN LIFE

- At age 4, success is not peeing your pants.
- At age 12, success is having friends.
- At age 16, success is having a driver's license.
- At age 20, success is having sex.
- At age 35, success is having money.
- At age 50, success is having more money.
- At age 60, success is having sex.
- At age 70, success is having a driver's license.
- At age 75, success is having friends.
- At age 80, success is not peeing your pants.

Three old women are sitting in the lounge of their retirement residence reminiscing about old times.

"I can remember buying a cucumber this big for five cents," one woman says, holding up her hands to demonstrate how long and thick the cucumber was.

> "I'm 59 and people call me middle-aged. How many 118-year-olds do you know?"
>
> –Barry Cryer

The second woman says, "Onions used to be much cheaper and bigger back then, too," she says, holding up her hands to indicate how big they were. "I can remember when you could buy two enormous onions like this for just 10 cents."

The third woman says, "I can't hear a word you two are saying, but I think I remember the guy you're talking about."

A grandmother is telling her granddaughter about her childhood. "Yes," she says, "back in my day we used to skate every winter on a frozen pond. We picked wild raspberries in the summer, and we even had our own pony."

"Wow, Grandma," says the young girl, "I wish I'd got to know you sooner."

HOW OLD HIT SONGS COULD BE UPDATED FOR AGING BOOMERS

- Mrs. Brown You've Got a Lovely Walker (Herman's Hermits)
- I Get By with a Little Help from My Depends (Ringo Starr)
- You Can't Always Pee When You Want (The Rolling Stones)
- How Can You Mend a Broken Hip? (The Bee Gees)
- Hello, I Love You. Won't You Tell Me My Name? (The Doors)
- Bad Prune Rising (Credence Clearwater Revival)
- Bald Thing (The Who)
- Splish Splash I Was Havin' a Flush (Bobby Darrin)
- I Am Woman, Here Me Snore (Helen Reddy)
- You're So Varicose Vein (Carly Simon)
- You Make Me Feel Like Napping (Leo Sayer)
- The First Time Ever I Forgot Your Face (Roberta Flack)
- Fifty Ways to Lose Your Liver (Paul Simon)
- Dream a Little Dream of Pee (Cass Elliot)
- You Don't Want to See My Naked Body (Leonard Cohen)
- Once, Twice, Three Times to the Bathroom (The Commodores)
- Heard It Through the Grape Nuts (Marvin Gaye)
- Denture Queen (Abba)
- A Whiter Shade of Hair (Procol Harem)
- Papa's Got a Kidney Stone (The Temptations)
- It's My Procedure and I'll Cry If I Want To (Leslie Gore)
- On the Commode Again (Willie Nelson)

YOU KNOW YOU'RE
AN AGING HIPPIE IF...

- your hair still contains a fully functioning eco-system
- your children are all named after celestial objects
- the question, "What's your favorite Grateful Dead song?" takes you five minutes to answer
- when attending a funeral, you automatically light a joint after the eulogy
- you still carry a picture of Gandhi in your wallet
- there are people you consider "family," yet you don't know their last names
- you're still getting pulled over by the cops and searched, even though you're an old gray-haired guy, and you are white
- most of your furniture consists of bean bags
- out of habit, you pass your cigarette to whom-ever is sitting beside you
- you have children with names like Bud, Herb or Mary Jane
- you can roll perfect cigarettes with one hand
- you think "All You Need Is Love" was written by Gandhi
- people you've never met before come up to you and ask if you can score them some weed

Q: What do you get when you play New Age music backward?

A: New Age music.

TEN QUALITIES A BOOMER WOMAN EXPECTS IN A MAN

When she's young, idealistic and single:

1. He must be handsome.
2. He must be charming.
3. He must be financially successful.
4. He must be caring, attentive and a good listener.
5. He must be tall, lean and in good shape.
6. He must be witty.
7. He must dress stylishly.
8. He must appreciate the better things in life, such as art, music and fine cuisine.
9. He should be creative, intelligent and full of surprises.
10. He absolutely must be an imaginative and romantic lover.

When she's a bit older, wiser and willing to accept reality:

1. He'll pass as long as her friends agree that he's "not too ugly."
2. His habits are acceptable to her as long as he's reminded not to fart or scratch himself in public.
3. He more or less works steadily.
4. He doesn't nod off when she's emoting.
5. He's in good enough physical condition to rearrange the furniture once in a while.

6. He usually remembers the punch lines to his jokes, except when he's been drinking.

7. He usually manages to wear matching socks and sometimes even remembers to change his underwear after he showers.

8. He knows enough not to buy champagne that comes with a screw-on cap, and never to buy wine that comes in a box.

9. He remembers to put the toilet seat down more often than not.

10. He makes at least rudimentary attempts at foreplay, and seldom does annoying things like beating his chest with his fists and yelling "Me Tarzan, you Jane" after he orgasms.

When she's middle-aged and has endured numerous failed relationships:

1. He's a "catch" so long as he can still carry a few groceries with ease.

2. He seldom forgets her name.

3. He's not in serious debt and doesn't require much money for upkeep.

4. He usually remembers to wear some clothes when lounging around the house.

5. He owns at least one tie.

6. He remembers where the bathroom is.

7. He usually remembers where he left his teeth.

8. He owns at least one shirt that covers his belly.

9. He remembers why he is laughing.

10. He seldom drives off before she gets into the car.

When she's old and gray and doddery herself:

1. He's in good enough shape to stand by himself.
2. He doesn't scare small children.
3. He doesn't miss the toilet too often.
4. He'll pass as an acceptable partner as long as he still has a pulse.

THE BOOMER MAN'S LAMENT

Back in my youth, when I was about 15 or so, I longed for the day when I'd find a girlfriend with really big boobs. At that time, all I thought I wanted in a woman was ginormous breasts, and I became obsessed with the idea.

By the time I was 18, I thought I'd found my dream girl—she had a fantastic body, great legs, was a sexy dresser, and, most important of all, she had by far the biggest boobs in my high school. But before long, I grew tired of her. She was no fun to be with, and there was no passion in our relationship. Apart from her gorgeous body, she was a total zero.

By the time I was 20, I decided that big boobs weren't really all that important to me any more, and what I really needed was a passionate girl with a zest for life.

In my second year of university, I dated a very affectionate girl who was a lot of fun to spend time with and was really great looking. She was willing and responsive, and for several months we enjoyed lots of hot and heavy imaginative sex. She was really into me, and for a while, I thought I'd found the woman of my dreams. But then, as luck would have it, I eventually grew tired of her, too. She was far too emotional for me. She was a total drama queen; everything in her life was one frantic disaster after another. Life with her was an emotional roller coaster. She went from laughing hysterically one minute to crying like a baby the next.

So that was when I decided that I needed a more stable partner. At the age of 30, I found a very down-to-earth, level-headed girl. She was methodical and totally predictable in her habits, and she never got excited about anything. But before long, I noticed that life with her was way too dull, and what I really needed was a girl with some spark, someone who was totally alive.

So then I found a really exciting girl, who seldom sat still and rushed from one thing to another, never settling on anything. She laughed at all my jokes and was a fantastic lover. But she did crazy impetuous things that drove me nuts. At first, she was great fun to be with because she was so energetic

> "When I was young, I was called a rugged individualist. When I was in my fifties I was considered eccentric. Here I am doing and saying the same things I did then, and I'm labeled senile."
>
> –George Burns

and unpredictable. But soon I found that I couldn't keep up with her and I began to hate her wild, directionless ways.

So I decided to find a girl with some ambition, someone with purpose in her life. When I was 39, I met a smart, aggressive woman who had her feet planted firmly on the ground. She wanted a big house and lots of kids, and I thought she'd be a great mother and a real inspiration for our children. She had a fabulous job, loads of drive and wanted to be vice president of the company she worked for. So I married her. But she turned out to be so ambitious that she eventually left me to marry the president of her company. She divorced me, took our kids, our house, my car and pretty much everything else I owned.

Older and wiser now, I'm a 52-year-old guy back out cruising the bars every night, looking for a young girl with really big boobs.

Q: Why did the hippies call them "roach clips"?

A: Because "pot holder" was already taken.

REASONS TO BE THANKFUL THAT YOU'RE NOW AN AGING BOOMER

- No one expects you to rush, run, hurry up, exert yourself or even show up on time—for anything.

- You're no longer of any value to kidnappers. In a hostage situation, you are likely to be released first.

- You'll get to eat a lot of free food and drink loads of free booze at your friends' funerals.

- Things you buy now will probably never wear out.

- No one will think you're weird if you eat dinner at 5:00 PM.

- If there's a sex maniac on the loose in your neighborhood, you are not likely to be a suspect.

- Instead of worrying about the shape of your boobs, you worry about them banging against your knees.

- If you're single, as long as you don't smell permanently of urine, you'll be considered a "catch."

- Your investment in extra health and dental insurance is finally paying off.

- You can butt into lineups and get away with it by telling the pretty young girl behind you that you're "old and confused."

- You can get away with being drunk, obnoxious and abusive at family gatherings because your relatives now dismiss you as "just a character."

- No one will expect you to run into a burning building to save the occupant.

- You can enjoy exchanging horrific stories with your friends about your operations and theirs.

- There's nothing left to learn the hard way.

- Your secrets are safe with your aging friends because they can't remember anything, either.

A group of 40-year-old fraternity brothers get together to discuss where they should hold their reunion dinner. They think it would be fun to hold the event at the Excelsior Bistro because they've heard the place has really friendly, sexy waitresses who wear skimpy little skirts and low-cut blouses.

Ten years later, the 50-year-old men meet again to discuss their reunion dinner, and again they go to the Excelsior Bistro because they've heard that the food is still good and that the place has one of the best wine lists in town.

Another decade goes by; the now 60-year-old fraternity brothers meet again to discuss their reunion, and once again they go to the Excelsior Bistro because it's known to be a quiet place and is smoke-free.

At 70 years of age, the group meets again to plan their reunion, and again they decide to go to the Excelsior because it's wheelchair accessible and it has an elevator.

Another decade goes by; the now 80-year-old members meet again and unanimously agree to have their reunion at the Excelsior Bistro because they've all heard it's good, and none of them remembers having been there before.

⚔ CHAPTER THREE ➤
Defying Gravity

Cynthia is a Baby Boomer who takes great pride in her appearance. After having numerous facelifts as well as umpteen nips and tucks all over her body, she has convinced herself that she looks much, much younger than her peers.

One day, she visits a different cosmetic surgeon to see if he can shave a few more years off her face. As she sits in his waiting room, she happens to notice that the doctor's name is spelled out in full on a diploma on the wall. Cynthia observes that it is the same name as that of a guy she'd had the hots for in high school, and she wonders if he could possibly be the same guy she had an enormous crush on way back then.

> "I had plastic surgery last week. I cut up my credit cards."
>
> –Henny Youngman

The cosmetic surgeon turns out to be a balding, pot-bellied old guy with frizzy gray hair and warts and wrinkles all over his face. At first, Cynthia thinks there's no way this could be the same handsome young dude she remembers from high school. But when she asks him if he attended Central High, he replies, "Yes, I did."

And when she asks him what year he graduated, he says, "1965."

Upon hearing this, Cynthia replies, "Well, I'll be damned, you were in my class!"

The guy looks Cynthia straight in the eye and says, "Oh yeah? What did you teach?"

On her 50th birthday, Julie decides to treat herself and have major cosmetic surgery. She goes to one of the top plastic surgeons in her city and orders a major overhaul: boob job, nose job, face lift, liposuction on her tummy and buttocks—the works.

After all of her surgery is completed, she thinks she looks great. She buys some new clothes and heads out into the world, proud to show off her new, rejuvenated face and body.

> "I bought a new wrinkle cream. If you use it once a day, you'll look younger in a month. Twice a day, and you'll look younger in two weeks. I ate it."
>
> –Rita Rudner

Her first stop is at a local Starbucks. When she gets to the front of the line, she asks the barista to guess how old she is.

"I'd say you're about 35," says the guy.

"No, I'm 50," says Julie, with a sly wink.

Next, she goes into a drugstore to pick up a prescription. She says to the pharmacist, "How old do you think I am?

He says, "Oh, I'm guessing you're not a day over 30," says the druggist.

"Well, actually I'm 50," says Julie, grinning proudly.

Julie then goes to a bus stop, and while standing inside the shelter, she turns to an old man seated alone on the bench. "How old do you think I am?" she says, confident that the wizened old guy will guess that she's still in her 20s.

"You can't fool me," says the old man. "I have a sure-fire method of guessing a woman's age. If you'll just let me put my hands under your bra, I'll bet you $100 that I can guess exactly how old you are."

By now, Julie is so confident about the success of her surgery that she decides to take the old man up on his bet. She loosens her bra and lets the old guy slip his hands under her sweater. He feels her breasts for a few seconds and examines them carefully. Then he announces proudly, "You're exactly 50 years old!"

> "She got her looks from her father—he's a plastic surgeon."
>
> –Groucho Marx

"That's amazing!" says Julie. "How did you do that?"

"It was easy," replies the old guy. "I was behind you in the line at Starbucks."

Linda is a very flat-chested Boomer woman who tells her husband that she would like to get breast implants.

"We can't afford them," says her husband. "Why don't you just try rubbing wads of toilet paper up and down between your boobs?"

"Do you think that will make them bigger?" asks Linda.

The husband replies, "Well, it worked on your ass."

Sandra is an aging Boomer woman who goes to her plastic surgeon for the umpteenth time to see if he can remove a new batch of wrinkles on her face.

"The secret of staying young is to live honestly, eat slowly and lie about your age."

–Lucille Ball

"I'll do the best I can to remove them," says the surgeon, "but I'm not making any promises. You've had six facelifts already."

After she awakens from the surgery, Sandra discovers that she's been given enormous breast implants.

"Why did you do this?" she asks the surgeon. "All I wanted was a few wrinkles removed, and now I have huge boobs."

"I couldn't do another facelift," replies the surgeon. "So I figured if I gave you big boobs, nobody will notice your wrinkles!"

YOU KNOW YOU'VE HAD TOO MUCH COSMETIC SURGERY WHEN...

- your doctor informs you that you have the rarest blood type of all: Botox negative

- the skin on your face is so thin that you are often mistaken for a space alien

- the smooth, wrinkle-free skin on your face and neck that you've paid big bucks for has just made your head look like a condom stretched over a pumpkin

- you notice that you haven't been able to "raise an eyebrow" since 1992

- for you, keeping "a stiff upper lip" extends to your forehead, cheeks, nose and chin

- the term "say it with a straight face" no longer means anything to you—you say everything with a straight face

- you join a new social networking site called facelift.com

- your eyebrows disappeared long ago into your hairline

- the brand-new "cute little button nose" you're so proud of is really your navel

- your plastic surgeon informs you that the bags under your eyes that you want him to remove are, in fact, your boobs

- your plastic surgeon warns you that if he pulls your forehead up any higher, you'll be sporting a goatee

A flat-chested middle-aged woman goes to a doctor who advertises that he has a guaranteed method of enlarging a woman's breasts without surgery.

The doctor explains to her that his method involves the power of positive thinking. He says, "Every morning you must rub your chest up and down and repeat out loud, 'Scooby doobie doobies, I want bigger boobies.' Do that 10 times every day for a year, and I guarantee you'll get bigger breasts."

> "A woman went to a plastic surgeon and asked him to make her like Bo Derek. He gave her a lobotomy."
>
> –Joan Rivers

The woman follows his advice, and, to her amazement, within three months the size of her breasts doubles.

One morning she is running late and forgets to do her boob enlarging ritual. Fearing she'll loose her big breasts, she stands on a crowded train rubbing her chest up and down and repeating out loud, "Scooby doobie doobies, I want bigger boobies."

A guy standing next to her leans over and says, "Excuse me, but would you happen to be a patient of Dr. McMillan?"

"Why, yes I am," says the woman. "How did you know?"

The guy leans over and whispers, "Hickory dickory dock…"

Two women are talking about their parents' declining health and the poor service they receive from the government-run health care programs they rely on. One woman says, "Can you believe it, my 65-year-old mother has waited almost a whole year for her operation?"

"That's deplorable," says the other woman. "The government should be ashamed to treat old people like that."

"Yeah, I know," says the first woman. "It's got to the point that the other day I said to her, 'Mom, do you really think it's necessary to get bigger boobs at your age?'"

Sally is a middle-aged woman with a serious heart condition. One night, she suffers a massive heart attack and is rushed to hospital in an ambulance. Surgeons work on her for several hours, and she almost dies on the operating table.

> "I don't plan to grow old gracefully. I plan to have facelifts until my ears meet."
>
> –Rita Rudner

In fact, she comes so close to dying that as she is walking toward the light, she meets God.

"Is this it for me, God?" she asks. "Is this the part where the curtain falls for the last time and I'm meeting my maker?"

"No, Sally," replies God, "your life is far from over. I can assure you that you have many years ahead of you. So go back and enjoy your life; it will be a long, long time before we meet again."

Sally regains consciousness and recovers quickly. Within days she feels great and has a new lease on life. She decides to live her life to the fullest, and treats herself to some expensive cosmetic surgery, including a facelift, a tummy tuck and breast implants—the works. She also dyes her hair and buys a complete new wardrobe.

Then one day she steps off a curb and is run over by a bus. She dies, goes to heaven, and once again meets God. "What's up with this, God?" she says. "It's me, Sally. Remember me? A couple of months ago you told me I had many years ahead of me. And now I'm back here again. What gives?"

God squints his eyes and replies, "Geez, sorry about that, Sally. I guess I just didn't recognize you."

Bertha goes into the hospital to undergo plastic surgery. She is lying naked on a hospital bed with her body covered by a single sheet as a nurse pushes her down the corridor to the operating room.

When the nurse leaves Bertha for a few minutes to check to see if the surgeons are ready, a young man in a white coat walks up to Bertha, lifts the

"I'd like to grow old with my face moving."

–Kate Winslet

sheet, examines her body, then lowers the sheet and walks away.

Bertha sees the guy talking to a second man, also wearing white coat, and he, too, walks up to her, pulls back the sheet, examines her body, then walks away and talks to a third guy in a white coat. The three men have an animated discussion that ends with the third guy going up to Bertha, pulling back the sheet and examining her body, too.

> "We are all interested in the future, for that is where you and I are going to spend the rest of our lives."
>
> –The Amazing Criswell

This time she says to the guy, "Look, I appreciate all the concern and interest and the examinations and everything, but when are you going to start my operation?"

"I have no idea," replies the guy, "we're just here to paint the corridor."

An older Boomer couple is getting ready for bed. The woman is naked, standing in front of a full-length mirror. "As I stare into this mirror," she says, "I barely recognize myself anymore. My face is wrinkled, my boobs hang down to my waist, my arms and legs are flabby, and my ass looks like two deflated balloons."

She turns to her husband and says, "Please tell me just one positive thing about my body so I can feel better about myself."

The husband stares at her critically and says, "Well, there's certainly nothing wrong with your eyesight."

Jerry is a Boomer guy who gets severely injured in a car accident. In addition to numerous cuts, bruises and broken bones, his genitals are badly mangled in the crash. A plastic surgeon is called in, and he tells Jerry that it will be possible to repair his organ to look and work as normal, but he warns him that the cost of the procedure will not be covered by his insurance.

> "Retirement at 65 is ridiculous. When I was 65 I still had pimples."
>
> –George Burns

"You have three choices," says the doctor. "I can give you a small penis for $3500, a medium-sized one for $6500, or I can make a large one for you for $10,000."

Jerry thinks he would like at least a medium-sized one, or maybe even a large one, given that there is only a $3500 difference in price. "I'm thinking I'd like the biggest one you can make for me," he tells the doctor.

The doctor advises him to go home and talk about it with his wife before making his decision. "It's a very personal choice," says the doctor. "You don't want to get one that will disappoint her, but on the other hand, you don't want one that's so large that it will make her uncomfortable. It's the sort of decision you really need to make together."

> "Money can't buy you happiness, but it can pay for plastic surgery."
>
> –Joan Rivers

A few days later, Jerry is back in the plastic surgeon's office.

"What have you decided to do?" asks the doctor.

Jerry replies, "We've decided to remodel our kitchen."

✍ CHAPTER FOUR ✎

The Viagra Monologues

Q: If Tylenol's generic name is acetaminophen, Aleve's is anaproxen and Advil's is ibuprofen, what will the generic version of Viagra be called?

A: Mydixadrupin. (Or maybe mycoxafloppin. Or perhaps mydixadud. Or maybe a simpler name that suggests a solution to the problem would be better, such as dixafix or mydixarizen or even ibepoken.)

Q: What are the ingredients in Viagra?

A: Three percent vitamin E, two percent aspirin, one percent vitamin C, five percent spray starch and 89 percent Fix-a-Flat.

Government studies show that over the past 10 years, more money has been spent on Viagra and breast implants than was spent on Alzheimer's research. It's estimated that if this trend continues, by 2025 there will be millions of old people walking around with enormous erections and really big breasts—and no one will remember what to do with them.

An old guy goes into a drugstore and asks the pharmacist if they stock Viagra.

"Of course we do," says the pharmacist. "Do you have a prescription?"

"No, I don't," says the old guy, "but would a picture of my wife do?"

Two Boomer guys, Sam and Mel, are having lunch, and Sam says, "You know, when you get to our age, you should always eat lots of rye bread. It'll help you maintain better, firmer erections."

"Really?" says Mel, "I didn't know that. I'll have to try some."

On the way home, Mel stops by his local bakery and asks for a loaf of rye bread.

"Do you want it whole or sliced?" asks the baker.

"What's the difference?" asks Mel.

> "Everything that goes up must come down. But there is a time when not everything that's down can come up."
>
> –George Burns

"Well," says the baker, "if you get it sliced, it'll get hard sooner."

Mel replies, "How come everyone knows this stuff except me?"

An old guy goes into a large medical clinic to see a urologist. The waiting room is crowded, and there is a long lineup of people checking in with the receptionist, who is an unpleasant, ugly woman with a brusque manner and a bad attitude.

When he reaches the front of the line and gives the receptionist his name, she says in a loud voice, "OH YES, YOU'RE HERE TO SEE THE DOCTOR ABOUT YOUR IMPOTENCE PROBLEM, IS THAT RIGHT?"

All the other patients look up at the embarrassed old guy. Thinking fast, he replies in an equally loud voice, "NO, I'M HERE TO INQUIRE ABOUT A SEX CHANGE OPERATION—AND I'D LIKE THE SAME DOCTOR WHO DID YOURS!"

Q: What's the name of the new version of Viagra that's been developed to increase vaginal wetness?

A: Niagra.

A Boomer woman complains to her doctor about her husband's flagging libido. The doctor suggests they try Viagra, but the woman explains that her husband won't take any medications, not even aspirin.

"Just slip one pill in his coffee when he isn't looking," says the doctor, who writes her a prescription.

Several days later, the lady goes back to see the doctor, who asks her how the Viagra worked.

"Oh, my God!" says the woman. "You should've warned me! It was horrible what happened."

"Was the sex not good?" asks the doctor.

"The sex was fantastic," says the woman. "Best in years."

"So what went wrong?" asks the doctor."

"I dropped one of those Viagras in his coffee just like you said," says the woman,

> "I have outlived my dick."
>
> –Willie Nelson (on the occasion of his 75th birthday)

"and then this enormous bulge appeared in his pants. He stared at me like a thing possessed, and then with one sweep of his arm he cleared the table, sending the coffee cups flying. Then he tore off all my clothes and ravished me on the table right there and then."

"The pills worked exactly as I told you they would," says the doctor. "So what was so awful?

"They work too fast," replies the woman. "I don't think I'll ever be able to show my face in Starbucks again!"

Q: Why is Viagra like Disneyland?

A: You have to wait an hour for a three-minute ride.

Herman is down on his knees praying one night while his wife gets ready for bed.

"What are you praying for?" asks his wife.

"Guidance," replies Herman, "guidance."

"I've got a better idea," says the wife. "Pray for stiffness—I'll guide it myself."

> "I'm taking Viagra and drinking prune juice. I don't know whether I'm coming or going."
>
> –Rodney Dangerfield

"Do you want breakfast?" asks a Boomer woman to her older husband.

"Nah," replies the husband. "The Viagra makes me lose my appetite."

A while later, the wife asks, "Do you want lunch?"

"No," replies the husband. "I've lost my appetite because of the Viagra."

Still later, the wife says, "How about dinner?"

"No, I don't want anything," says the husband. "It's the Viagra—I just don't have any appetite."

"Well, what about me?" replies the wife. "Would you mind getting the hell off me for a minute so I can get something to eat?"

Q: What do Chinese men take before elections?

A: Viagla.

Casper goes to his doctor and complains that his wife has lost all interest in sex.

"You gotta help me, doc," he says. "I'm desperate. Is there a pill or something I can give her?"

The doctor replies, "I can't prescribe anything for someone who is not my patient."

"Aw, c'mon, doc," says Casper. "I'm gonna go crazy if you don't help me."

The doctor then reaches into his desk drawer and pulls out a bottle of pills. "Ordinarily, I wouldn't do this," he says. "These pills are an experimental version of Viagra for women. Tests indicate that they're very powerful. I'll let you try them if you promise me that you won't give her more than one at a time, understand? Just one."

"OK, but are you sure one will be enough?" asks Casper. "She's awfully cold."

"Trust me, one pill will do the trick," replies the doctor. "Don't push your luck."

That night, after dinner, when Casper's wife goes out of the room, he drops one of the female Viagra pills into her coffee. Then, remembering what an iceberg his wife is, he decides that a second pill might really do the trick for him, so he drops another one into her coffee for good measure.

But then he feels guilty. He remembers that the doctor warned him that the pills were powerful and that he should give her only one pill at a time. Casper decides to even things up a bit, and so he takes one pill himself.

Twenty minutes later, he notices a strange look on his wife's face. She comes over and sits down beside him and whispers in his ear, "I need a man."

Then Casper suddenly begins to feel funny all over, and in a trembling voice says, "Me too."

Q: What's the difference between a Catholic Boomer woman and a Jewish Boomer woman?"

A: The Catholic Boomer tells her husband to buy Viagra. The Jewish woman tells her husband to buy Pfizer.

A man goes into a drugstore and gets his first prescription for Viagra. He takes the pills home and knocks one back immediately, and then sits down to wait for his wife to come home.

Meanwhile, his pet parrot sees the pills on the kitchen counter and goes over to the open package and takes one himself. He likes the taste, so he eats another, and another, until the whole package is gone.

When the guy sees the huge erection on the parrot, he stuffs the bird into the freezer to cool it off. Then, as luck would have it, the old man's wife comes home just as the Viagra kicks in, and he rushes her upstairs to try out the new drug.

> "If my dick was as stiff as my knees, I'd be in great shape."
>
> –Ronnie Hawkins

Two hours later, he remembers the parrot, and goes to the freezer to let him out. Expecting the worst, he is relieved to find the bird covered with sweat and totally exhausted.

"What happened?" asks the guy. "You were in the freezer for two hours and now you're sweating like crazy."

The parrot replies, "Have you ever tried to pry apart the legs of a frozen chicken?"

Q: Have you heard about the new cereal for impotent men?

A: It's called Nut 'n' Raisin Honey.

A 10-year-old boy walks to his grandparents' house one day and notices that his grandpa is sitting on the porch with nothing on from the waist down.

"Grandpa!" yells the kid, "why are you sitting outside with no pants on?"

"Well, sonny," says the old man, "the other day I sat out here with no shirt on and I got a stiff neck… let's just say this is your grandmother's idea."

Q: What's the difference between anxiety and panic?

A: Anxiety occurs when, for the first time, you can't do it a second time. Panic occurs when, for the second time, you can't do it the first time.

Hubert is sitting in his doctor's office. "I've got a big problem," he says to the doctor. "I'm really worried about my penis."

"What's the matter with it?" asks the doctor.

"Well, when I was a young lad and it got hard, I couldn't bend it," explains Hubert. "Then, when I was in my 40s, I remember I could bend it a little bit. Now I'm in my 60s, and when it's hard, I can bend it a lot."

"So what do you want me to do to help you?" asks the doctor.

"Doc," says Hubert, "please tell me I'm getting stronger."

A dentist is about to pull out an old man's tooth.

"Do you want a needle to numb the pain?" the dentist asks the man.

"I'm afraid of needles," says the geezer. "I don't want one."

"How about some gas to put you under?" asks the dentist.

"No way," says the old guy. "I'm allergic to gas."

The dentist then hands the man a pill and says, "Take this."

"What is it?" asks the guy.

"Viagra," replies the dentist.

"What good will Viagra do?" asks the patient. "Will it ease the pain?"

"No, it won't," replies the dentist. "But at least it will give you something to hold onto while I yank this tooth."

A 75-year-old guy goes into a drugstore to fill his prescription for Viagra. After the pharmacist counts out the pills, the old guy asks him to cut each one into four pieces.

"It won't do you much good if you take it in such small doses," warns the druggist.

"Oh no, I don't want it for sex," says the old guy. "I just want it to stick out far enough so that I don't pee on my shoes."

Q: What happens when a lawyer takes Viagra?

A: His head swells up, and he grows fatter and taller.

Two elderly widowers are talking about Viagra. One guy says, "Now that I'm over 70, I can get all the Viagra I want from my new drug program, for free. Isn't that great?"

The other guy says, "Yeah, that's great. But what's the point of putting lead in your pencil if you have no one worth writing to?"

A guy goes into a drugstore and says to the pharmacist, "Do you have Viagra?"

"Yes, we do," replies the pharmacist.

"Can I get it over the counter?" asks the guy.

"You sure can," replies the pharmacist, "if you take two of 'em!"

Q: Have you heard about the new Viagra for men with back problems?

A: It combines Viagra with the ingredients in Robaxacet, so your back won't peter out and your peter won't back out.

A woman goes to visit her father, who lives in a nursing home. She asks, "How are you feeling, Dad?"

"Oh, much better," replies the old man. "I'm getting a lot more sleep since they started giving me a glass of warm milk and a Viagra every night at bedtime."

The woman says nothing and just thinks her father is getting confused again, but before she leaves the home, she stops by the nurses' station. "My father tells me that you're giving him a glass of milk and a Viagra every night at bedtime." she says. "Is he getting confused about his medications again?"

> "Just because you're an old dog doesn't mean you can't bury your bone."
>
> –Willie Nelson

"No, he isn't," says the nurse. "The warm milk helps him sleep, and the Viagra keeps him from rolling out of bed."

An old man goes to his doctor and asks for the strongest dose of Viagra available. "I'm spending the weekend with two young nymphomaniacs," he says, "so I want the real potent stuff."

The following Monday, the guy is back at the doctor's. This time he asks him for painkillers.

> "I'm at the age where I want two girls. If I fall asleep, they will have someone to talk to."
>
> –Rodney Dangerfield

"Are these for your penis?" the doctor asks as he writes the prescription.

"No, they're for my wrist," replies the man. "The women didn't show up."

Henry and Doris are a couple who live together in a nursing home. They are sitting in their wheelchairs one evening when Henry turns to Doris and says, "Can you help me do up my pajamas properly? My willy is sticking out."

Doris looks at Henry and says, "Don't flatter yourself, dear, your willy is just hanging out."

A Boomer guy goes on a business trip to Texas, where he buys an expensive pair of snakeskin cowboy boots. When he gets home, he wants to show them off to his wife, so he strips naked except for the cowboy boots.

"You notice anything special?" he asks.

"No, it's limp as usual," says the wife.

"It's not limp," replies the guy, "it's admiring my new boots."

His wife replies, "Next time, buy a hat."

An older man falls asleep on a Florida beach and gets a second-degree sunburn over his entire body. He is rushed to hospital where he is treated for painful blisters.

The head doctor on duty says to the nurse, "Put him on intravenous feeding with a saline solution containing electrolytes and a sedative. And I want you to give him a Viagra every four hours."

"Viagra?" says the nurse. "What use is Viagra to soothe his burns?"

"Viagra will help him a lot," replies the doctor. "It'll keep the sheet off his body."

Q: Do you know what the makers of Viagra call
    Cialis and Levitra?

A: Stiff competition.

A married guy goes to his doctor and complains
about his impotence problem. The doctor gives
him a prescription for Viagra. "This should do the
trick," he says the doctor. "Come back and see me
in two weeks."

Two weeks later, the guy returns to the doctor's
office. "That Viagra stuff you gave me is fantastic,"
he says. "It's a miracle. I just want to thank you for
giving it to me."

"No problem," says the doctor. "I'm glad to hear
it. By the way, what does your wife think of it?"

"Wife?" replies the man. "Oh, I haven't been
home yet."

CHAPTER FIVE

Little Romances

A couple in their 60s visits a sex therapist. The husband says, "We want you to watch us having sex."

The therapist thinks the request is a bit odd, but he agrees. When the couple is finished, the therapist says, "You're both fine. There's nothing wrong with either of you. That will be $75."

The couple pays the therapist and leaves. A week later, they call and make another appointment. They come in, make out on the therapist's couch while he watches them, pay him the $75 fee, and leave.

This goes on week after week, and each time, the therapist collects his $75 fee and tells them they are fine and that there is nothing he can do to help them improve their sex lives.

One day a few months later, the therapist says, "What exactly to you hope to accomplish with these sessions?"

The guy replies, "We don't expect to accomplish anything. Truth is, we can't afford to go anywhere else."

"What do you mean?" asks the therapist.

"Well," says the guy, "here's our problem: she's married, so we can't go to her house. I'm married, too, so we can't go to mine. The Hilton charges

$200, and the Holiday Inn costs $150. If we do it in your office, you charge us just $75, and I get $60 back from my health insurance."

A man in his early 30s meets a middle-aged woman in a bar. They talk for a while and flirt a bit, and after a few drinks, the guy starts to think the older woman is pretty hot for someone he figures must be in her mid to late 50s.

After several more drinks, they exchange a passionate kiss, after which the woman whispers in the man's ear, "Have you ever had sex with a mother and a daughter together?"

"No, I haven't," replies the guy, "but to tell you the truth, it's something I've fantasized about all my life."

"Well, then this could be your lucky night," purrs the woman while giving him a sly wink. "Why don't we go back to my place?"

They leave the bar arm-in-arm. The guy can hardly contain his excitement as they kiss some more in his car and again on the doorstep before entering the woman's house.

"Are you ready for the time of your life?" she asks as she unlocks the door.

"Oh, God, yes, I am," replies the man. "Let's go in and do it."

The woman opens the door and they enter her house. Then she flicks on the light and yells upstairs, "Mom, are you still awake?"

An old woman finds a brass lamp on a Florida beach. She takes it home and cleans it up, and as she is polishing it, a genie pops out of the lamp. "Thank you for releasing me from my prison," the genie says. "As your reward for setting me free, I will grant you three wishes."

> "Oh, to be 70 again!"
>
> —Oliver Wendell Holmes
> (upon seeing an attractive woman on his 95th birthday)

The woman thinks for a moment and replies, "Okay, for my first wish, I want to be young and beautiful again." POOF! She is transformed into a 20-year-old beauty.

"For my second wish, I would like five million dollars," she says. POOF! Five million dollars appear on her table.

"And for my third wish," she says, "I'd like you to transform my old cat over there into my handsome prince charming." POOF! The cat magically becomes a handsome young man.

When the genie leaves, the handsome young man turns to the beautiful young woman and says, "Now I'll bet you're sorry you got me neutered."

Old Harry is at his doctor's office getting a physical. His doctor asks him, "Are you still sexually active?"

"You bet your boots I am, doc," replies Harry. "Why, in the past six months, I've slept with four different women, and, I might add, every one of 'em was under the age of 30."

> "I can remember when the air was clean and sex was dirty."
>
> –George Burns

"That's amazing for a man of your age," says the doctor. "I hope you at least took some precautions."

"Look, I might be old, but I'm not stupid," says Harry. "I gave 'em each a phony name."

A widowed woman puts an ad in the personals column of the local newspaper to find a new mate. She specifies that she has three requirements:

(1) The man must be kind and gentle.

(2) He must be stable and want a quiet home life.

(3) He must be a good lover.

One day her doorbell rings and she opens her door to find an old guy with no arms or legs sitting in a wheelchair. "I'm here in reply to your ad," he says.

"And do you meet all the qualifications I specified?" asks the woman.

"Oh yes, I most certainly do," replies the guy. "Look, I have no arms, so I can't be abusive or mistreat you. And I have no legs, so I can't run off on you."

"But with no arms or legs, how can I be sure you'll be any good in bed?" asks the woman.

"Think about it," replies the old guy. "How do you think I rang your doorbell?"

An older Boomer guy goes out one night to the local red light district and tries to pick up a prostitute. He walks up and down the street and eventually strikes up a conversation with a young hooker. The woman thinks he's crazy and gives him the brush-off.

"Get lost, you senile old fart," she says. "You're ruining business for me."

"But I want to get laid," replies the old man.

"You've got to be joking," says the hooker. "You're past it. You're finished!"

"What did you say?" asks the old man, leaning closer.

"I said, you're finished!" says the hooker.

"Oh, okay," says the old guy. "How much do I owe you?"

An old lady walks into the dining room of her nursing home, raises a clenched fist in the air and yells, "If any of you guys can guess what's in my hand, you can have sex with me tonight!"

One old guy yells out, "It's a refrigerator!"

The women thinks for a moment and replies, "Close enough."

A widowed Boomer woman is sitting on a park bench in Arizona. An old guy wanders by and sits down on the same bench.

"Are you a stranger around here?" she asks.

"Oh, I used to live here about 10 years ago," says the guy.

"Where have you been for the past 10 years?" asks the woman.

"In prison," says the guy.

"What did you do?" asks the widow.

"I murdered my wife," replies the guy.

"Oh my," says the old woman, "so you're a single man then…"

A 66-year-old man goes to the doctor for a checkup. After examining him, the doctor says, "You're in great shape for your age. Tell me, how old was your father when he died?"

The patient replies, "Did I say my father is dead?"

The doctor is astonished. "You've got to be kidding me. Your father is still alive? So, tell me then, how old was your grandfather when he died?" he asks.

The patient replies, "Did I say my grandfather is dead?"

"Wow, that's really incredible," says the doctor. "You're 66 years old and you have a father and a grandfather who are both still alive!"

"Not only that," replies the patient, "but last week my 108-year-old grandfather got married for the first time."

> "Love is the answer, but while you're waiting for the answer, sex raises some pretty good questions."
>
> –Woody Allen

"Amazing," says the doctor. "But tell me, after 108 years of bachelorhood, why did your grandfather want to get married now?"

The old man replies, "Did I say he wanted to?"

An older Boomer woman sees a sign in a Montreal pet store window that says: "Clitoris-licking Frog Needs Good Home."

She goes into the store and says to the clerk, "I'm interested in the clitoris-licking frog."

The clerk replies, "Oui, madame, c'est moi..."

A wealthy 69-year-old man is having coffee with an old friend. "I've got big news," he says, "I'm going to marry that hot little 22-year-old I've been dating."

The friend says, "You're a lucky man. But tell me, how did you convince such a gorgeous young woman to marry you?"

"I lied to her about my age," says the old guy. "I told her I'm 96."

A middle-aged guy is walking through a super-market one day when he notices a pretty young woman is smiling and waving at him. "Hi, there," she says as she walks up to him. "Do you remember me?"

"Do I know you?" says the man.

> "A man is as old as the woman he feels."
>
> –Groucho Marx

"I'm pretty sure you do," says the woman. "I think you're the father of one of my kids."

Panic-stricken, the guy stares at the woman for a few moments, frantically trying to remember her from all of the women he has slept with over the years. Then, it dawns on him.

"Oh, yeah, I remember you," he says. "Aren't you the stripper who performed at my stag party? The one who wore the kinky leather outfit and asked me to whip you and tie you down with rope and then let me bang you on the pool table while all the other guys watched? Was that you?"

"No," replies the woman, "I'm your son's history teacher."

Bernice and Larry are in their 60s and thinking about getting married.

"I want to keep my house," says Bernice.

"That's okay by me," says Larry.

"And I want to keep my BMW," says Bernice.

"No problem," says Larry.

"And I want wild, passionate sex six times a week," says Bernice.

"Fine by me," says Larry. "Put me down for Fridays."

A man and woman who have never met before find themselves assigned to the same sleeping compartment on a transcontinental train.

Although they are a little embarrassed about sharing the same room, the two are tired and both of them fall asleep, he in the upper bunk and she in the lower.

In the middle of the night, the guy awakens, reaches down, taps the woman on the shoulder and says, "Sorry to bother you, but would you mind reaching in the closet and handing me an extra blanket? I'm freezing up here."

"I've got a better idea," the woman says. "Just for tonight, let's pretend that we're married."

"Oh, yeah!" says the man. "That's a great idea."

"Good," says the woman. "Then get up off your lazy ass and get a goddamn blanket yourself."

The guy climbs down, takes a blanket from the cupboard and crawls back up into his bunk. Then, just like the old married guy he is pretending to be, he lets out an enormous fart and falls back to sleep.

An old guy takes a fancy to an elderly woman he meets on a cruise ship. He decides to ply her with booze in the hope that he might get lucky. The old lady is flattered by all the attention she is getting, and before long, the two are quite loaded. They end up back in the old lady's room grinding it out in the sack.

"My God, you're still tight," says the old man after he finishes. "If I'd known that you were still a virgin, I'd have been more gentle."

The woman replies, "If I'd known that you could still get it up, I'd have taken off my panty hose."

A teenaged girl comes down from her room to wait for her date. Her grandmother walks by her and notices that the girl is wearing a see-through blouse and no bra.

"That's no way for a young woman to dress when she's going out on a date," says the older woman.

"Relax, Grandma," says the girl. "This is the way kids dress today. Ya gotta let your rosebuds show!"

> "Men are like fine wine. They start out as grapes and it's up to the woman to stomp the crap out of them until they turn into something acceptable to have dinner with."
>
> –Dave Barry

The next evening, the teenager comes downstairs to find her grandmother sitting on the sofa with no shirt on. The sight of her granny sitting in the living room topless freaks her out.

"You can't sit there like that," she says. "My boyfriend will be here any minute."

"Relax," says the grandmother, "if you can show off your rosebuds, then I can display my hanging baskets."

An old guy walks into an exclusive jewelry store with a shapely young woman on his arm. "We'd like to purchase that diamond necklace in the window," he says to the clerk. "How much is it?"

"Twenty thousand dollars," replies the clerk.

"Fine, wrap it up," says the man. "Will a check be okay?"

"Sure," says the clerk. "But we'll have to wait a few days for it to clear. Can you come back on Monday to pick up the necklace?"

"No problem," says the old guy as he writes the $20,000 check. "We'll see you then."

The old guy and the young woman gleefully walk out of the store arm-in-arm.

"People ask me what I'd most appreciate getting for my 87th birthday. I tell them a paternity suit."

–George Burns

The following Monday, the old guy returns to the store alone. The clerk confronts him and says, "That check you gave us bounced. I'm surprised you have the nerve to come back here."

"Sorry about that," says the old guy. "I came back to apologize and to thank you for the best weekend of my life."

An old woman tells her doctor that she wants an HIV test. The doctor asks her why she thinks she needs it, considering her advanced age.

She says, "I heard on TV that everyone should be tested after having annual sex."

Bill and Angie are two aging Boomers who have been dating for several weeks. One night they go out on the town, have dinner and a few drinks, and go back to Angie's. Things progress to the point that they end up in her bedroom for the first time.

Bill watches intently as Angie undresses in front of him. First, she takes out her false teeth and puts them in a glass. Then off comes her dress. Bill notices that she has a prosthetic leg, and he watches as she removes it and rests it against the wall. Next, she removes her bra, and two falsies tumble out onto the floor. Then she pops out a glass eye and carefully places it in a little box on her night table. Finally, to his dismay, he watches as she takes off her wig and tosses it onto a bedpost.

Noticing that Bill has yet to undress, Angie says, "Don't just stand there. What are you waiting for?"

Depressed by what he has just witnessed, Bill replies, "You know what I want. Why don't you just take it off and throw it over here?"

An old married guy is sitting at a roulette table in Las Vegas, when a hot-looking young hooker sits down beside him. They strike up a conversation, and when the hooker eventually propositions him, out of curiosity he asks her how much she charges.

"Two hundred dollars an hour," she says proudly.

"Wow," replies the guy, "I'd never spend that much for sex."

"So," says the hooker, "how much would you spend?"

"Fifty bucks, tops," he replies.

"Well, so long," says the hooker. "You won't get much action in this town for $50."

Later that evening, the guy is strolling back to his hotel room with his wife when he passes the same hooker in the hall. She leans over and whispers in his ear, "See what I mean? That's what you get for $50 in Las Vegas."

A 75-year-old woman goes out on a date with an 80-year-old man.

When she returns home later in the evening, her daughter asks her why she is so upset.

"What happened?" asks the daughter.

"Oh, it was awful," says the old woman. "I had to slap his face three times."

"Did he try to get fresh with you?" asks the daughter.

"No," says the old lady. "I thought he was dead."

Two old guys get really drunk one night in a bar. On their way home, they pass by a brothel, and in their drunken stupor, they stagger in. The madam in charge sees the sorry state the two old guys are in and sends them upstairs to two rooms she has set aside for drunks—each of the rooms has a life-sized inflatable doll on the bed.

The next morning, the two men sober up in a nearby coffee shop and talk about their big night in the brothel.

"I think the woman in my room was dead," says George.

"Why do you say that?" asks Dave.

"She never moaned or groaned or nothin'," says George. "She just lay there like a beached whale."

"I think mine was a witch," replies Dave.

"My God," says George, "what makes you think that?"

"Well, I wasn't getting much response from mine, either, so I thought I'd try out my new false teeth. So I bit one of her boobs and still got no response."

"But what makes you think she was a witch?" says George.

"'Cause when I bit her boob a second time, all she did was fart real loud…and then she flew out the window."

> "Whenever I date a guy, I think, is this the man I want my children to spend their weekends with?"
>
> –Rita Rudner

Hillary and John are an older couple who are thinking about getting married. They are talking about their future together, and after they discuss finances, living arrangements, wedding plans and so on, John brings up the subject of sex.

"How often do you want it?" he asks.

Hillary replies, "I would like it infrequently."

John says, "Is that one word or two?"

A middle-aged guy bumps into his ex-wife one day in a supermarket. After a brief conversation, he says, "Why don't we go back to my place and tear one off the way we used to?"

His ex-wife replies, "Over my dead body!"

The guy replies, "Like I said, just the way we used to."

An older couple who have been dating for six months decide to get married. One day they are walking past a drugstore, and they go in to speak to the pharmacist.

"Excuse me," says the guy, "but I wonder if you could help us. Are you the owner of this store?"

"Well, yes," says the pharmacist, "as a matter of fact I am."

"Great," says the old man, "we just have a few questions. First, do you sell walkers, canes and wheelchairs?"

"Yes, we do," says the pharmacist.

"Okay," says the guy, "then how about medications for heart disease, poor circulation, arthritis, scoliosis, jaundice, colitis and enlarged prostate?"

"Yes," says the pharmacist, "we have all of that."

"Okay," says the old man, "how about Viagra, suppositories and enemas?"

"Oh, yes," replies the pharmacist, "we have all of those, too."

"Fantastic," says the guy. "How about adult diapers, sleeping pills and medications for irritable bowel syndrome?"

"Yup," says the pharmacist, "we've got all of those."

"Great!" replies the old man. "We'd like to register here for all our wedding gifts."

Ninety-year-old Harold is sitting in the garden of his nursing home talking about aging to Wilma, an 81-year-old woman he has just met. "The thing I miss most," he tells her, "is sex."

"You silly old fart," replies Wilma, "I'll bet you couldn't get it up if your life depended on it."

"Well, maybe not," says Harold. "But sometimes I think it would be nice if a woman would just hold it for a while."

"I'd be happy to do that for you," says Wilma.

So Harold unzips his fly and Wilma slips her hand inside his pants and grasps his manhood. They sit like this for an hour or more, and then agree to meet again the following night.

There in the garden once again, he unzips his fly and Wilma slides her hand inside his pants and holds his organ for over an hour. They both enjoy this intimacy so much that they agree to meet secretly in the garden every night for the following week.

Then one night Harold doesn't show up. Wilma searches all over for him and eventually hears that he is sitting in the garden with another woman.

The next day she confronts Harold. "What's the attraction to that woman?" she asks. "Is she younger than me?"

"No," says Harold.

"Is she prettier than me?" she asks tearfully.

"No, she's not," says Harold.

"Then what has she got that I don't have?"

Harold sheepishly replies, "Parkinson's."

⪻ CHAPTER SIX ⪼
Until Death Do Us Part

After 30 years of marriage, a couple goes to a family counselor to try to resolve a number of issues that the woman feels are threatening their relationship.

For the first 20 minutes, the wife pours out her heart in an emotional tirade expressing her grief. She tearfully explains how she feels neglected, alone and unloved, how she longs for more intimacy in their relationship, how desperately she desires more passion and physical contact, and wails on and on describing her many other unmet needs.

At the end of all this, the therapist gets up from his seat, walks around his desk and asks the woman to stand up. He embraces her firmly and then gives her a long and very passionate kiss on the lips, while her husband sits and watches intently.

When the therapist releases the woman from his embrace, he turns to the husband and says, "There, that's what your wife needs, at least three times a week. Can you do this?"

The husband thinks for a moment and says, "Well, I can certainly drop her off here on Mondays and Wednesdays, but on Fridays, I play golf."

A retired Boomer guy says to his wife, "I never want to live in a vegetative state, dependent on some machine and a bunch of fluids drained into me out of a bottle. If that happens to me, I want you to just pull the plug."

So his wife gets up off the couch, unplugs the TV and pours his beer down the sink.

Betty and her husband Bob share the same birthday and have been married for 40 years. On their 65th birthdays, a fairy appears before them and grants them each one wish.

Betty says, "I'd like to spend a month in Hawaii." And POOF! Two tickets to Maui magically appear in her hands.

> "My wife and I were happy for 20 years. Then we met."
>
> –Rodney Dangerfield

Bob says, "I'd like to have a woman 30 years younger than me." And POOF! He becomes 95.

An old lady goes to see a lawyer and tells him that she wants to start divorce proceedings against her husband.

The lawyer asks, "How old are you?"

"I'm 84," says the woman.

"And how old is your husband?" asks the lawyer.

"He's 87," replies the old lady.

"And how long have you two been married?"

"Sixty-two years," says the woman.

"My goodness," says the lawyer, "Sixty-two years is a long time. Why do you want a divorce now?"

The old lady frowns and calmly stares at the lawyer and says, "Enough is enough."

Q: Why do Boomer women close their eyes during sex?

A: Because they can't stand to see their husbands having a good time.

Harriet and Wilfred have been married for 40 years. They are lying in bed one night, and just before they drift off to sleep, Wilfred reaches over to Harriet and begins to fondle her in ways he hasn't done in quite some time.

First, he caresses her shoulders and neck, and then runs his hand down her spine to the small of her back. Then he slowly slips his hand up along her left side and caresses her breasts. Next, he gently slides his hand across her stomach and down the outside of her left thigh. His hand then moves up the inside of her thigh and gently roams down her right leg to her knee, where it stops briefly then slowly works its way back up the outside of her leg to her abdomen. Then Wilfred stops, rolls over and is silent.

"That felt wonderful," Harriet coos, "but why did you stop?"

He says, "I found the remote."

Marie and her husband Jake are aging Boomers who decide to celebrate their 35th wedding anniversary by going to the same hotel and staying in the same room they had on their wedding night. As they prepare for bed, Marie strips naked, stands in front of Jake and says, "What were you thinking when you first saw me like this 35 years ago tonight?"

Jake thinks for a moment and replies, "I was thinking how much I wanted to screw your brains out."

"And what are you thinking now?" asks Marie.

Jake says, "I'm thinking I did a pretty good job."

Lucille comes home and says to her husband, "Did you hear old Joe Taylor died yesterday?

Isn't that terrible? He and Jennifer had been married for only two months."

Her husband replies, "Oh well, he didn't suffer for too long then."

An old couple is having a terrible argument about who is to blame for their lousy love life. The husband screams, "When you die, I'm gonna get you a headstone that reads, 'Here Lies My Wife—Cold As Ever'!"

"Oh, yeah?" yells the wife. "Well, then I'm gonna get you a headstone that reads, 'Here Lies My Husband—Stiff At Last'!"

An older Boomer man is sitting on a park bench crying. A cop walks by and stops to check if the guy is okay.

"Are you all right, sir?" asks the cop. "Why are you so upset?"

"I just got married," sobs the man. "I married a wonderful woman who is 25 years younger than me."

> "Getting married for sex is like buying a 747 for the free peanuts."
>
> –Jeff Foxworthy

"So things are not working out?" says the cop.

"Oh, no," says the man. "We're very happy. I have a fantastic life with my new bride. She really loves me and looks after me. She makes my breakfast and serves it to me in bed every morning. Then we bathe together and make love. In the evenings, she prepares fantastic dinners for me, and then we retire early every night for more lovemaking."

"Well," says the cop, "it sounds to me like you have a great life."

"Oh, I do," says the man.

"So what is making you so sad?" asks the cop.

The old man bursts into tears again and says, "I can't remember where I live."

Q: Why do Jewish men usually die before their wives?

A: Because they want to.

A 67-year-old man rushes to the hospital when he hears that his 36-year-old wife has gone into labor. A nurse greets him with the news that his wife has just given birth to twins.

"That just proves what I've always said," says the guy. "Even though there's snow on the roof, there's still fire in the furnace."

"If that's true," replies the nurse, "then I think you'd better change your filter because both your kids came out black."

Jocelyn turns to her husband one day and says, "Whatever happened to our sexual relations?"

The husband thinks for a moment and replies, "Yeah, I don't think we even get a Christmas card from them any more."

A man from New Orleans goes into a government office to apply for Social Security. He waits in line for a long time, and when he finally hands his application to the government clerk, she asks him for some identification.

"I seem to have left my wallet at home," says the guy, frantically searching through his pockets. "Don't I look 65?"

"Yes, you do," says the clerk. "Tell you what, just unbutton your shirt, and if I see a lot of curly gray hairs on your chest, that'll be proof enough for me that you're 65."

The guy unbuttons his shirt and shows off a great forest of gray hair. The clerk agrees that he must be 65 and processes his application.

Later that day, the man goes home and tells his wife what happened—how he opened his shirt and the clerk accepted his claim based on the gray hairs on his chest.

"You should have dropped your pants as well," she says. "You could qualify for disability, too."

Two older women, Annabel and Jane, are having coffee. Jane says, "How is your husband holding up in bed these days?"

Annabel says, "Let's put it this way. Lately he makes me feel like an exercise bike."

"How so?" asks Jane.

"He climbs on and starts pumping," says Annabel, "but we never get anywhere."

Frida and Garry are a Boomer couple who are lying in bed one night when Garry starts to make some moves on her. She pushes him away and says, "I don't feel like it right now; I just want you to hold me."

"Aw, c'mon, honey," says Garry, "just a little—"

"No," says Frida, "I told you I just want you to hold me right now. That's all I want. You've got to try to be more in tune with my emotional needs as a woman."

Garry holds his wife for a while and then falls asleep.

The next day, he takes his wife out shopping. They go into a department store, where she tries on three expensive outfits and asks him which one he likes the best. "Take all three of them," he says.

Then they go to the shoe department and she looks at three pairs that will complement the outfits she has chosen. "Get all three of 'em," Garry says, with a wave of his hand.

By now, Frida is jumping up and down with excitement. When they pass the jewelry department, she stops to look at an expensive diamond necklace. "It would look great on you," says Garry. "Why don't you try it on, and while we're here, why don't you pick out some earrings to match?"

> "Sex is better when you're older, because we don't have to change our sheets. The nurses do it for us."
>
> –Joan Rivers

"Okay, I think I'm finished now," says Frida. "Let's go to the cash register and pay for—"

"Oh no, NO!" says Garry. "We're not going to buy all this stuff. I just want you to hold it for a while."

Frida stares at him blankly.

Garry says, "You've got to try to be more in tune with my financial needs as a man."

A couple in their 60s is sitting on their sofa one evening watching television. Suddenly, without warning, the old man reaches over and cuffs his wife on the back of her head.

"What was that for?" she screeches.

"That's for 42 years of lousy sex," he replies.

> "In my house, I'm the boss; my wife is just the decision maker."
>
> –Woody Allen

A few minutes later, the wife reaches over and cuffs her husband on the back of the head.

"Why did you do that?" he asks.

She replies, "That's for knowing the difference."

Q: How are Boomer women like hurricanes?

A: When they come they are loud and wet, and when they leave, they take your house and car.

An old couple is sitting in a train station. The guy says, "I hate it when the trains are late. I've been sitting here so long my ass has fallen asleep."

"I know," replies his wife. "I can hear it snoring."

A slightly senile man is sitting with his wife in his doctor's office. The doctor explains that he needs to do some tests. "I'll require a blood sample, a urine sample and a stool sample," says the doctor.

"How am I going to do all that?" asks the old man.

His wife replies, "Just give him a pair of your underpants."

A bellhop greets a married Boomer couple who have just checked in to a first-class hotel. "Good afternoon, sir," says the bellhop. "Can I carry your bag for you?"

"Nah," replies the old guy, "she can walk."

A Boomer couple is driving along a snow-covered highway when they spot an injured skunk at the side of the road. They stop, and the wife gets out and brings the skunk into the car.

"It's cold and shivering; what should I do with it?" she asks her husband.

"You could try to warm it up by putting it between your legs," he replies.

"What about the smell?" she asks.

The husband replies, "Hold its nose."

An 75-year-old guy marries a 25-year-old woman. On their wedding night, the bride decides that they should have separate rooms in case her aged husband needs more rest than she does.

Shortly after she settles down in her room, there is a knock on the door. Her new husband comes in, slips into her bed, has sex with her, kisses her good night then returns to his room across the hall.

Ten minutes later, there is another knock on her door. To her surprise and delight, it is her new husband. She lets him in, and once again they have sex, after which he gets up and returns to his room.

Another 15 minutes go by, and there is yet another knock on the door. It's her husband again, and this time he rushes in, gives her a big wet kiss and pushes her down on the bed.

"Wow!" says the young bride. "I'm really impressed with your stamina. It's amazing to me that a guy your age is up for it three times in one hour."

"Huh?" replies the old man. "Have I been in here before?"

A couple is arguing about the type of vehicle they should buy. The husband wants a shiny new pickup truck; his wife wants a snazzy little sports car.

"I don't care about the make or model," she says. "I just want something that will go from

0 to 200 in seconds. My 65th birthday is coming up in a few weeks, so surprise me."

When her birthday arrives, the husband goes out and buys her a new bathroom scale.

An old guy goes to the doctor and tells him that after 30 years of marriage to the same woman, he can't get an erection any more. The doctor tells him to make another appointment and to bring his wife with him.

A week later, the man returns with his wife. The doctor tells her to go into his examination room and to take off all of her clothes, and tells the husband to wait outside. She follows his instructions, and when she is completely naked, the doctor enters the room, walks around her and examines her from all angles.

He then goes out of the room to speak to the husband and says, "Relax. You have nothing to worry about. You're fine. There's absolutely nothing wrong with you."

"Really?" says the husband. "How can you be so certain?"

The doctor replies, "She doesn't give me a hard-on either."

An aging couple is lying in bed. Just as the husband is falling asleep, the wife says, "You used to hold my hand in bed." So the guy reaches over and holds her hand.

A few minutes later she says, "You used to kiss me good night before we went to sleep." So her husband leans over and gives her a peck on the cheek, then tries to settle down to sleep.

"You used to bite my neck and nibble my ears," she says. The guy throws the covers back and springs out of bed.

"Where are you going?" she asks.

He replies, "To get my goddamned teeth."

An old man goes up to his wife, pinches her ass and says, "You know, if you firmed this up, we could get rid of all your control-top pantyhose."

Then he slips his hand under her sweater, fondles her boobs and says, "You know, if you firmed these up a bit, we could get rid of all your bras."

The wife spins around, grabs his crotch and says, "If you firmed this up we could get rid of the gardener, the pool boy, the mailman and your brother."

A Boomer couple have six kids, and the husband is so proud of all the children he has fathered that he begins calling his wife "Mother of Six," despite her objections.

All day long she hears it: "Mother of Six, get the kids ready for school." "Mother of Six, it's time to make dinner." "It's your turn to put the kids to bed, Mother of Six." And so on.

> "Marriage is like a coffin, and each kid is another nail."
>
> –Homer Simpson

One night the couple goes to a party. They both have a lot to drink, and the husband is really getting on the wife's nerves by calling her Mother of Six in front of their friends: "Mother of Six, let's dance." "Mother of Six, do ya want another drink?"

By the end of the evening, she loses it. When her husband says, "Hey, Mother of Six, I think it's time we went home," she snaps back, "Okay, Father of Two, let's go."

Q: What's the difference between an ex-wife and a catfish?

A: One is a scum-sucking bottom feeder, and the other is a fish.

Winnie is going a bit deaf and is also starting to get confused. One day she asks her doctor if there's any chance that she'll get pregnant again.

"You're 63 years old," replies the doctor. "You can never rule out an act of God, but if you were to have a baby, it would be a miracle."

When she arrives home later that day, Winnie's husband asks her what the doctor said.

"Oh, I think my doctor is losing his mind," she replies. "I didn't quite catch everything he said, but it sure sounded fishy to me…something about an act of God and if I had a baby it would be a mackerel."

A Boomer couple goes to the doctor for their annual physical examinations. The doctor examines the husband first, and after checking him over, he asks him if he has any concerns.

"I've got a really unusual sex problem," says the guy. "After the wife and I have sex the first time, I'm really hot and sweaty. But after the second time, I'm cold and shivery. What can this mean?"

"That's interesting," says the doctor. "I'll look into it."

The doctor calls the man's wife in, and while he is examining her, he says, "Your husband tells me that when you have sex the first time, he's hot and

> "I love being married. It's so great to find that one special person you want to annoy for the rest of your life."
>
> –Rita Rudner

sweaty, and the second time, he's cold and shivery. Do you have any idea what his problem is?"

"Oh, he's just a silly old fart," replies the woman. "It's because the first time we have sex is usually in July, and the second time is in December."

Lorne and his wife Louise are an older couple sitting in their dentist's waiting room. When the dentist comes out, Lorne jumps to his feet and says, "Okay, here's the deal, doc. I've got two buddies waiting for me at the golf course, so I'm in a big hurry. Forget the anesthetic—just pull this tooth real quick, and we're outta here."

"You've got to be kidding me," says the dentist. "Are you sure you want me to pull a tooth without using any painkillers?"

"Aw, c'mon," says Lorne. "Let's just get on with it. There's no time to wait for the anesthetic to work. Just pull the sucker out, and we'll be on our way."

"Well, okay," says the dentist. "Which tooth is it?"

Lorne turns to Louise and says, "Okay, honey, open your mouth real wide and show him."

Marilyn and Larry are Boomers who have been married for 30 years. Marilyn has always thought it odd that for the entire duration of their marriage, Larry has insisted they make love in total darkness, but because he is a fantastic lover who never fails to satisfy her, she goes along and never complains.

One night while they are having sex, her curiosity gets the better of her. At the height of her orgasm, she reaches over and switches on a light and is shocked to discover that he is using a vibrating dildo on her. "Larry!" she shouts. "How do you explain this?"

"I'll explain this," says Larry, "if you can explain to me how we have two kids."

An older couple is watching a faith healer on television. The televangelist tells his viewers to put one hand on their television and the other hand on the part of their body that they want healed. So the wife gets up, walks over to the TV and puts her left hand on it and her right hand on her arthritic knee.

Then her husband gets up, walks over and puts one hand on the TV and the other on his crotch.

The wife says, "Fer Chrissakes, Bert, he said he can only cure our ailments, not raise the dead."

Albert wants to get his much younger wife pregnant, so he goes to his doctor to have a sperm-count test. The doctor gives him a specimen cup and tells him to take it home, fill it and return it the next day.

Albert shows up the next day with the specimen cup, still empty and with the lid still on it.

"I've got a real problem," he says to his doctor. "I tried my right hand, and got nowhere. Then my left hand...nothing. My wife tried with her right hand...still nothing. Her left hand...no luck either. She even tried putting it in her mouth...still nothing. Then my daughter tried: right hand, left hand, her mouth...still nothing."

> "Never go to bed mad. Stay up and fight."
>
> –Phyllis Diller

"Wait a minute," says the doctor. "You mean you asked your own daughter to—"

"Yeah," says Albert, "none of us could get the lid off the specimen cup!"

A 95-year-old couple goes to a lawyer and tells him that after 75 year of marriage, they want a divorce.

The lawyer asks, "Why did you wait so long?"

The woman says, "We wanted to wait until our kids were dead."

A man goes into a bar and orders a double scotch. And another. And another. When he goes to order a fourth drink, the bartender says, "You drink like a man with a problem."

> "I haven't spoken to my wife in years. I didn't want to interrupt her."
>
> –Rodney Dangerfield

"Boy, do I," says the man. "I've been married for 42 years, and today I came home and found my wife in bed with my best friend."

"That's terrible," says the bartender. "What did you say?"

The guy replies, "BAD DOG, BAD DOG!"

Q: How does an aging Boomer know if his wife is dead?

A: The sex is the same, but the dishes pile up.

Enid is a middle-aged woman who is having lunch with her old friend, Becky. "My husband has lost all interest in sex," she says. "I don't know what I'm going to do."

Becky says, "Have you tried wearing a sexy nightie?"

"Yes, I have," replies Enid. "I have one with a really low front and an even lower back. He used to go crazy when he saw me in it."

"So here's what to do," says Becky. "Try to mix it up a bit. Try putting it on backward. Then it'll be even more daring because the back plunges lower than the front. That might turn him on."

That night Enid follows Becky's advice. She goes into the bathroom, takes off all her clothes and slips on the nightgown front to back. She walks into the bedroom, spins around and says, "Honey, do you notice anything different tonight?"

Her husband glances up from his book and says, "Yeah, tonight the skid marks are on the front."

Sixty-year-old Myrtle wakes up one morning and says to her husband, "Joe, I think I'm dead."

Joe replies, "No, you're not, Myrtle. You're lying here talking to me."

"No," says Myrtle, "I'm dead."

"Why do you think you're dead?" asks Joe.

Myrtle looks around, still dazed and confused, and says, "Because nothing hurts."

A couple married for over 30 years is having an argument. The wife screams, "I WAS A FOOL WHEN I MARRIED YOU!"

The husband replies calmly, "Yes, dear, but I was young and in love and I didn't notice."

An older couple is sitting on the front porch in their rocking chairs. After a long silence, the old guy turns to his wife and says, "Ma, I think I've got an erection."

After an even longer silence, the old lady says, "So what do you think you're going to do with it, Pa?"

Another long silence. Eventually the old man replies, "I dunno." He sits quietly for a while longer then turns to his wife and says, "You know, I've been thinkin'…"

"Ya, Pa?" says the wife, hopefully.

"Yeah," says the husband. "I've got an idea."

"What is it, Pa?" asks the wife in eager anticipation.

"I'm thinkin'," says the old man, "now that I've got the wrinkles out, it might be a good idea to go upstairs and wash it."

"A good wife always forgives her husband when she's wrong."

–Milton Berle

Boomer Eric comes home after a long day on the golf course and says to his wife, "I've got a great idea. Tonight, let's change positions."

"Terrific," replies his wife. "You do the dishes, and I'll sit on the sofa and fart."

The CIA is testing the mettle of three new female recruits at their Washington headquarters. The trainer hands a gun to the youngest recruit, a 25-year-old trainee, and tells her that her husband is in a room at the end of a corridor and that she must go into the room and kill him.

"Forget it," she says. "I can't do it. I'm newly married, and I love my husband too much."

The trainer then hands the gun to an older recruit, a 35-year-old woman, and tells her she must go to another room down the hall where her husband is waiting, and kill him.

The 35-year-old agent goes into the room, but comes out after a few minutes and says, "Sorry, I just couldn't do it. We've only been married for five years; I love my husband too much."

Then the CIA trainer hands the gun to the oldest recruit, a 55-year-old woman, and instructs her to go into yet another room where she will find her husband, and to kill him.

The older woman storms down the hall and goes into the room. Three shots ring out in rapid succession, followed by a lot of screaming and scuffling. Finally there is silence, and the woman comes out with a crazed grin on her face.

"What the hell happened in there?" asks the trainer.

The woman replies, "Some asshole put blanks in the gun, so I had to strangle him."

Sixty-year-old Mildred returns from a visit to her doctor and says to her husband, "The doctor told me I have the body of a 25-year-old."

"What about your big ass?" asks the husband.

"Oh," replies Mildred, "your name never came up."

Emma is an older Boomer woman who thinks she's still kinda hot. She steps out of the shower one day and stands naked in front of her husband.

"What is it about me that turns you on most?" she asks him. "Is it my pretty face or is it my sexy body?"

Her husband replies, "It's your sense of humor."

A Boomer guy tells his doctor that his much younger wife is pregnant, even though he hasn't had sex with her in over a year.

"How can this be?" the old guy asks his doctor.

"It's what we in the medical profession call a grudge pregnancy," says the doctor.

"What's that?" asks the man.

"Well, simply put," says the doctor, "somebody's had it in for you."

Ed and Edith are about to celebrate their 40th wedding anniversary. "You know, 40 years ago we had a cheap apartment, a crummy old car and we slept on a sofa bed," says Ed. "But back then I got to have sex with a 25-year-old."

> "The only time my wife and I had a simultaneous orgasm was when the judge signed the divorce papers."
>
> –Woody Allen

"So what's your point?" asks Edith.

"Well, I've been thinking," says Ed. "Now we have a big house, a new car and a huge big bed, but now I'm sleeping with a 65-year-old woman. It just ain't fair."

"Okay," says Edith, "go find yourself a sexy 25-year-old. And if you do, I'll make sure you end up back in a cheap apartment, drive a crummy old car and sleep with her on a sofa bed."

Old Harry and his wife Mabel are sitting on the sofa watching television when suddenly Mabel says, "Let's go upstairs and have sex."

Harry thinks about it for a minute then replies, "I don't think I can do both."

Linda and Richard are a Boomer couple having dinner in a restaurant. Suddenly, a stunning young blonde walks up to Richard, plants a big kiss on his cheek and says, "See you later," then gives him a wink and disappears into the crowd.

"Who the hell is that?" asks Linda.

"She's my mistress," replies Richard.

"Oh, yeah?" says Linda. "Well, that's the last straw! I want a divorce!"

"I can understand why you'd say that," says Richard. "But just remember, if we divorce, there will be no more shopping trips to Paris, no more winters in Barbados, no more summers in Tuscany, no more BMWs or Lexuses in the garage and no more yacht club. But the decision is yours."

Just then, a mutual friend enters the restaurant with a gorgeous young woman on his arm.

"Who's that woman with James?" asks Linda.

"That's his mistress," replies Richard.

Linda says, "Ours is prettier."

Q: How does an aging Boomer tell if her husband is dead?

A: The sex is the same, but she gets the remote.

An aging Boomer guy sneaks up behind his wife and whispers in her ear, "How 'bout a quickie?"

She replies, "As opposed to what?"

Gerry and Louise are celebrating their 25th wedding anniversary. As the couple is about to cut their cake, old Gerry's eyes fill with tears.

"I didn't know you'd be so sentimental about this," says Louise. "I'm really touched."

"No, no," says Gerry, "I'm not being sentimental at all. I was just thinking about the time, way back when, your father caught us making out on your parents' back porch."

"Oh, yes," says Louise, "I remember that night like it was yesterday. I was only 15 years old and I got pregnant the very first time we did it."

"And do you remember how angry your father got, and how he told me to either marry you or spend the next 25 years in jail?"

"Yes, I remember," replies Louise, meekly.

"Well, it just occurred to me," says Gerry, "today I would be a free man."

A Boomer couple is on vacation. The husband sees a wishing well, walks up to it and throws in a coin. He stands there looking at it as it sinks to the bottom, but nothing happens.

Then his wife takes out a penny and walks up to the wishing well. She trips on a step, falls in and drowns.

The guy stares at the wishing well in disbelief and mutters to himself, "Holy shit, it works!"

WHY OLDER MEN THINK DOGS ARE MORE FUN THAN THEIR WIVES

- Dogs don't cry (unless they have to pee).
- Dogs love it when their owners' friends come over.
- Dogs don't care if their owners use their doggie shampoo.
- A dog's time in the bathroom is confined to a quick drink.
- Dogs don't expect their owners to call when they are running late. The later they come home, the more excited dogs are to see them.
- Dogs will forgive their owners for playing with other dogs, and they don't notice if they are called by another dog's name.
- Dogs don't shop.
- Dogs don't mind if their owners give away their offspring.
- Dogs think farts are funny, and they think their owners sing great.
- Anyone can get a good-looking dog. And if a dog is drop-dead gorgeous, other dogs don't hate her.
- Dogs like it when their owners leave stuff on the floor.
- Dogs never need to examine the relationship.
- A dog's parents never visit.
- Dogs understand that instincts are better than asking for directions.
- Dogs like beer.
- Dogs don't hate their bodies.
- No dog ever bought a CD by Celine Dion.

- No dog ever put on 100 pounds after reaching adulthood.
- Dogs appreciate excessive body hair.
- Dogs never criticize.
- Dogs agree that it's necessary to raise your voice to get your point across.
- Dogs never expect gifts.
- Dogs don't worry about germs.
- Dogs don't want to know about every other dog their owners ever had.
- Dogs like to do their snooping outside, as opposed to in their owner's wallet or desk.
- You never have to wait for a dog; they're ready to go 24 hours a day.
- Dogs think it's funny when their owners get drunk.
- Dogs can't talk.
- Dogs seldom outlive their owners.
- When a dog gets old and starts to snap at you incessantly, you can easily get rid of it.

A cop stops an elderly man who is driving erratically down a city street. The cop says, "Did you know that your wife fell out of your car three blocks back?"

"Thank God," the husband replies. "I thought I'd gone deaf."

WHY OLDER MEN THINK DOGS AND WIVES ARE ALIKE

- Both look stupid in hats.
- Both tend to have hip problems.
- Both look good in fur coats.
- Neither understands baseball.
- Both are good at pretending that they're listening to every word you say.
- Neither believes that silence is golden.
- Neither can balance a check book.
- Both put too much value on kissing.
- You can never tell what either of them is thinking.

WHY OLDER MEN THINK WIVES ARE BETTER THAN DOGS

- It's okay to have sex with a wife.
- Wives look good in sweaters.
- Wives leave the room to fart.
- Although they only have two, a wife's boobs are far more interesting.

Sylvia is a Boomer woman who is having terrible headaches every morning. A friend tells her about a hypnotist who cured her headache problem, and she suggests that Sylvia should see if he can help her.

Sylvia makes an appointment with the hypnotist. He instructs her to stand in front of a mirror and repeat 10 times every day, "I do not have a headache. I do not have a headache." She does this for a week, and to her amazement, the headaches disappear.

Thrilled with her success, Sylvia tells her husband, Jonathan, that he should see if the hypnotist can cure his flagging libido. Jonathan visits the hypnotist the next morning and comes home after his appointment, grabs Sylvia and pushes her into the bedroom. He tells her to take off her clothes and to get into bed, then he disappears into the bathroom. A few minutes later, he comes out, climbs into bed and they enjoy wild, passionate sex for the first time in months.

The next day, the same thing happens. Jonathan comes home after a golf game, grabs Sylvia, pushes her into the bedroom and then goes into the bathroom for several minutes. When he comes out, he jumps into bed with her and they have fantastic sex that is even better than the day before.

Sylvia is thrilled that the hypnotist has cured her husband's sex problem, but she wonders why he has to disappear into the bathroom for several minutes before they make love. So one night she sneaks up on him. She peers through the partially opened bathroom door and finds him standing in front of the mirror repeating over and over, "She is not my wife. She is not my wife...."

A middle-aged woman comes home one day and says to her husband, "Pack your bags. I just won five million dollars in the lottery."

"Wow," says her husband, "should I pack for a bus tour of Europe or a beach vacation in Hawaii?"

"I don't care where you go," says the wife, "just get the hell out."

A teenaged boy is talking to his grandfather about marriage. "Is it true that in some cultures a man doesn't know his wife until he marries her?" he asks.

The grandfather replies, "I'm afraid that happens in all cultures, son."

Alice says to her husband, Bill, "How many women have you slept with?"

"Only you, my darling," replies Bill. "With all the others I was awake."

After many years of marriage, a slightly senile old farmer from Oklahoma decides it's time to see a lawyer about getting a divorce.

"Do you have grounds?" says the lawyer.

"Yes, sir," replies the old man. "About 100 acres."

"No, no," says the lawyer, "I mean, do you have a case?"

"No, sir," says the old guy. "But I do have a John Deere."

"What I mean is, do you have a grudge?" says the lawyer.

"Yup," replies the farmer. "That's where I park my John Deere!"

"No, no, no," says the lawyer, who is becoming frustrated. "Do you have a suit?"

"Yessiree," says the old guy. "I wear it to church every Sunday."

"Does your wife beat you up?" asks the lawyer, trying another approach.

"Nope," says the farmer. "We both get up at the same time, 5:30 every morning."

"No," says the lawyer, "you don't understand. I'm trying to find out why you want a divorce. What does your wife think the problem is?"

The farmer thinks for a moment and replies, "She says she can't talk to me anymore."

On her wedding night, a 52-year-old bride turns to her new husband and says, "Please be gentle, I'm still a virgin."

"How the hell can you still be a virgin?" asks the husband. "You've been married three times before."

"Well," says the wife, "to understand me, you have to know about my previous marriages. My first husband was a gynecologist, and all he wanted to do was look at it. My second husband was a psychiatrist, and all he wanted to do was analyze it. Then there was my third husband. He was a clerk at the stamp counter in the post office, and all he wanted to do was lick... OH, GOD! I do miss him sometimes!"

> "I really wanted a child. I didn't want to be old and sick and not have someone to drain financially."
>
> –Rita Rudner

Tara and Ralph are two divorcees out on their first date together. While dining out in an upscale restaurant, Tara notices that Ralph keeps staring at a very drunk woman sitting a few tables away from them.

"Do you know her?" she asks.

"Yes, I do," replies Ralph. "She's my ex-wife. She took to drinking right after we got divorced seven years ago."

"My goodness!" says Tara. "Who would think that someone could go on celebrating that long?"

Sally is reading the morning newspaper while sitting across from her husband, Frank. "It says here that, on average, 50 percent of all marriages end in divorce," she says. "Imagine that, one-half of all marriages!"

"When you think about it, that's not so bad," says Frank. "That means the other 50 percent end in death."

Two guys are talking in a bar. One man says to the other, "You've been married for 46 years. That's amazing. Tell me, what is the secret of your success?"

"It's very simple," says the other guy. "We agreed many years ago that it's the man's job to make all the big decisions, and the woman's job to make all the little ones."

"Does that work?" says the other guy.

"You bet it does," says the old married guy. "After 46 years, we've never had one big decision."

Boomer Betty says to her doctor, "My husband has a habit of screaming when he ejaculates.

"So what's the problem?" asks the doctor.

Betty says, "He's keeping me awake."

Old Sam is sprawled out on the sofa watching the football game on TV and drinking beer. His wife Phyllis yells out from the kitchen, "How 'bout getting up off your lazy ass and changing the light bulb in the hall fixture for me?"

"I'm busy right now," replies Sam. "Anyway, does it look like I've got a General Electric logo on my forehead? I don't think so."

A few minutes later, Phyllis screams out from the kitchen, "The fridge is broken again. Probably another gasket has blown. How 'bout getting your sorry ass in here and replacing it!"

"Do I look like I've got Westinghouse written on my forehead?" replies Sam. "I don't think so."

"Oh, yeah? Well, listen to me, you lazy bum!" yells Phyllis. "The front steps need to be fixed, too. I could break my neck on those rotten old boards. When are you going to fix them?"

"Do I look like I've got Ace Lumber written on my forehead?" replies Sam. "I don't think so."

Sam can't stand to listen to any more nagging from his wife, so he gets up from the sofa and heads for the door. "I've had enough of this crap for one day," he says. "I'm going to the bar for some peace and quiet."

Six hours later, Sam returns home and sees that the front steps are repaired and the hall light has a new bulb. When he goes into the kitchen for a beer, he notices that the fridge is working fine, too. "How did you get all this stuff fixed?" he asks his wife.

"While you were out," replies Phyllis, "a nice young man came knocking on the door looking for odd jobs. He said he'd do the chores for free, and in exchange all I had to do was either go to bed with him or bake him a cake."

"So what kind of cake did you bake him?" asks Sam.

Phyllis grins and says, "Do you see Betty Crocker written on my forehead? I don't think so."

> "I wouldn't be caught dead marrying a woman old enough to be my wife."
>
> –Tony Curtis

Q: What's worse than a male chauvinist pig?

A: A Boomer woman who won't do what she's told.

A middle-aged woman is walking alone on a Hawaiian beach one day when she finds an urn in the sand. When she picks it up and brushes it off, a genie pops out and says, "Thank you for releasing me from this urn. For your reward, I will grant you three wishes."

"Wow," says the woman, "I've been really down on my luck lately; this is fantastic."

"But wait," says the genie. "Because it appears that I've washed up on a Hawaiian beach, I must strictly follow Hawaiian laws for genie wish-granting. First, I must ask you a few questions. Are you married?"

"Divorced," says the woman.

"That's too bad," says the genie. "This means that I have no choice but to give your ex-husband double whatever I give you. Sorry, but that's the law for genies working in Hawaii."

"Okay," says the woman. "For my first wish, I want five million dollars."

"So be it," says the genie. "But that means I must grant your ex 10 million dollars."

"Okay...I guess," says the woman. "Now, for my second wish, I'd like a big house overlooking the ocean here on Maui."

"Done," says the genie. "But I'll have to give your ex a house worth twice as much as yours."

"If you say so," says the woman. "Now for my third wish...you'll have to let me think about this for a minute...Okay, I've got it. For my third wish, I'd like you to give me a mild heart attack."

Old Sidney has a terrible gastric-release problem. Upon awakening each morning, he greets the new day with an enormous fart that wakes up his wife, Edna. His farts leave such a foul smell that sometimes Edna is forced to run to the window gasping for air.

"I can't take this anymore," she says to Sidney one day. "The smell is making me sick. You'd better see a doctor about this before you blow your insides out."

Sidney argues that he can't stop farting and that it's perfectly natural for a man of his age to need to break wind when he wakens each morning. He refuses to see a doctor about his problem.

Then one Thanksgiving morning, while Edna is preparing her turkey, a malicious thought occurs to her. She takes a bowl containing the bird's gizzards upstairs where Sidney is still sleeping soundly. She gently pulls the covers back and empties the contents of the bowl into his pajama bottoms.

Some time later, she hears Sidney wake up and let out his usual enormous fart. But this time it's followed by a loud scream and frantic footsteps as he runs to the bathroom. Edna can hardly contain her laughter. After years of torture, she finally got him back.

Twenty minutes later, Sidney comes downstairs with a look of horror on his face.

"Honey, you were right," he says. "All these years you warned me, and I didn't listen to you."

"What do you mean?" asks Edna innocently.

"You told me that one day I'd end up farting my guts out, and today it finally happened," he says. "But with the aid of some Vaseline, I think I got most of them back in."

Old Roscoe goes to a Victoria's Secret store to buy a Valentine's Day present for his wife. "Show me something really sheer," he says to the clerk.

The clerk shows him a sheer negligee with a $200 price tag. "That's not sheer enough," says Roscoe. "Show me another one."

The clerk brings out the sheerest negligee in the store. It costs $500, but when Roscoe sees how transparent it is, he eagerly buys it and has the clerk wrap it up.

Roscoe goes home and proudly gives the present to his wife and tells her to go upstairs and put it on to model it for him. But when she opens the box and sees the $500 price tag still attached to the garment, she decides that she won't wear it and will take it back and exchange it for something else. She thinks that because the negligee is so sheer, all she'll have to do is stand at the top of the stairs stark naked, and half-blind old Roscoe will never know the difference.

> "My wife has cut our lovemaking down to once a month, but I know two guys she's cut out entirely."
>
> –Rodney Dangerfield

She takes off all her clothes and strikes a provocative pose at the head of the stairs. "How do you like it?" she shouts down to Roscoe.

He looks up and says, "It looks fantastic, but for 500 bucks, you'd think they could have at least ironed it."

Two old friends meet on the street. One woman says to the other, "How's it going since Bill retired last month?"

"For him it's great," replies the other woman. "But for me, it's coping with twice as much husband on half as much pay."

A couple married for over 30 years is driving down the highway. They are having a terrible argument, and the husband is trying to keep his cool to avoid driving erratically. He keeps to the speed limit of 50 miles per hour.

"I don't care that we've been married for 30 years!" shrieks the wife. "I want a divorce!"

The husband increases the speed to 75 miles per hour.

"Don't try to talk me out of it!" screams the wife. "My mind's made up. I've been having an affair with your brother for the past five years, and now I know that I must leave you to be with him."

The husband increases the speed to 85 miles per hour.

"I want the house, too!" yells the wife. "I figure I deserve it for giving up my career to look after you and the kids."

The husband says nothing, but increases the speed to 100 miles per hour.

"I want the kids to live with me, and I want the car and at least $100,000 in cash, too," she adds.

The husband says nothing but increases the car's speed up to 120 miles per hour and aims it at a concrete overpass.

"Is there anything you want?" asks the wife.

"Nope, I've got everything I need," says the husband.

"What do you mean?" replies the wife. "I plan to take everything."

Then, just before they hit the overpass at 130 miles per hour, the husband yells, "I'VE GOT THE ONLY AIRBAG!"

≪ CHAPTER SEVEN ≫
Family Matters

Sloan is a middle-aged guy who regularly goes to his doctor to have his blood pressure checked. During one visit, the doctor says, "Your blood pressure has gone through the roof. You're a prime candidate for a massive heart attack if you don't do something about it."

Sloan says, "High blood pressure comes from my family; there isn't much I can do about it."

"Your mother's side or your father's?" asks the doctor.

"Neither," says Sloan. "It comes from my wife's family."

"That doesn't make sense," says the doctor. "It's impossible for you to get high blood pressure from your wife's family."

"Oh, yeah?" Sloan replies. "You should try spending a weekend with them."

A middle-aged guy comes home at dawn after working the night shift, crawls into bed and makes love to his wife. Afterward, when he goes downstairs to the kitchen to have breakfast, he is startled to find his wife standing there pouring coffee.

"How did you get down here so fast?" he asks. "Just a few minutes ago we were having sex."

"OH, MY GOD!" screams the wife. "You DIDN'T! That's my mother up there in our bed. She wasn't feeling well when she dropped by last night so I told her to lie down in our room. She fell asleep so I left her there all night."

The wife rushes upstairs to the bedroom. "Oh, Mother, I'm so sorry," she says. "I can't believe what happened. Why didn't you say something?"

"Well," says the old lady, "I haven't spoken to that asshole you married for 15 years, and I wasn't about to start now."

A grandfather is walking through a drugstore with his adolescent grandson. The young boy is looking at a display of condoms. The grandson asks, "What are these for, Grandpa?"

"Those are used to protect women from getting pregnant," the grandfather says matter-of-factly, hoping to change the subject.

"Okay," says the grandson, "but why do they come in packages of one, three and 12?"

"Well, there's a simple reason for that," says the grandfather, trying to think of a suitable answer for a youngster. "The packages containing one condom are for high school kids. They just need one on a Saturday night. The packages that contain three condoms are for college kids. They need one for Friday night, one for Saturday night and another for Sunday night. And the pack with

12 are for old married guys like me. One for January, one for February, one for March…"

Rachel is an older Jewish woman who is elated to hear that her 35-year-old daughter, Sophie, is finally getting married and returning home from Israel to settle down with her new husband.

"There's something you should know about my husband," says Sophie when she phones her mother with the news. "He's an Arab."

"Oy, that's not so good," replies Rachel.

"But, Mother," says Sophie, "he's an Arab sheik. He's filthy rich. And he's promised me that he'll move back to New York with me and buy me a big house. What's more, he promised me that he'll take care of you, too. He says he'll buy you a mansion of your own and make sure that you live in luxury beyond your wildest dreams for the rest of your days."

True to his word, the Arab sheik moves to New York and buys both his bride and his mother-in-law palatial homes in one of the city's upscale neighborhoods. Rachel is ecstatic with her new home, and she happily settles in to her newfound life of luxury.

Months go by, and one day Sophie shows up at Rachel's new house with bad news. "I've got a terrible problem with my husband," she says. "I'm at the end of my rope with some of his habits; I don't know what I'm going to do."

"What's the problem?" asks Rachel.

"All he wants to do is have anal sex," says Sophie. "That's the only way he likes it. I can't take it anymore. When we got married, my rectum was the size of a dime; now it's the size of a silver dollar."

Rachel replies, "So for 90 cents you're going to cause trouble?"

A Boomer guy is sitting in a biker bar. He is getting very drunk and boisterous. After consuming too many drinks, he yells out to a tough-looking young biker guy sitting across from him, "You know what, you little punk? I'm gonna tell you sumptin' an' you better goddamn well listen to me. So here's the deal...I've had sex with your mother hundreds of times."

The biker guy pays no attention.

A few minutes later, the old guy moves a little closer to the biker and says, "Just last night I had a hot date with your mother, and she was really, really easy, if you get my meaning."

Still, the biker ignores him and turns away.

Then the old guy walks right up to the biker and yells in his face, "In fact, I'd go as far to say that your mother is the best goddamn lay I've ever had in my entire life!"

Finally, the young biker turns and glares at the old man and says, "Fer Chrissakes, Dad, sober up and go home!"

A little boy rushes to the front door to greet his visiting grandmother. "I'm so happy to see you, Grandma," he says. "Now Daddy can do the trick he promised us."

"What trick is that?" asks the grandmother.

"Oh, it sounds so cool," says the kid. "I heard Daddy tell Mommy that he would climb the f**king wall if you came to visit us again."

> "My grandmother was a very tough woman. She buried three husbands, and two of them were just napping."
>
> –Rita Rudner

A woman says to her daughter, "I don't want you to think I have diabetes because I'm fat. I have diabetes because it runs in our family.

"No, Mom," the daughter replies, "you have diabetes because no one runs in our family."

Young Eddie goes up to his grandmother and asks, "How did the human race evolve?"

His grandmother replies, "God made Adam and Eve, they had children and we all descended from them."

Eddie asks his grandfather the same question and is surprised when he gets a completely different answer.

"We evolved from the apes," says the old man. "Yup, we came down from the trees. We are all descendants from the monkeys, gorillas and orangutans."

Eddie goes back to his grandmother and says, "How come you told me the human race was created by God, and Grandpa says we descended from monkeys?"

The old lady thinks about the question for a moment and replies, "I told you about my side of the family; your grandfather is talking about his."

An old man who walks with a cane gets on a crowded bus, and no one stands up to give him a seat. As the bus lurches forward, the old guy's cane slips and he falls flat on his face.

As he slowly gets back up to his feet, a teenaged boy sitting on a nearby seat says, "Hey, old man, you should put one o' them little rubber thingies on the end of your stick, and then it won't slip."

The old guy replies, "Yes, I know, and if your father had done the same thing a few years back, I'd have your goddamn seat today."

An adolescent boy asks his grandfather, "Grandpa, how many kinds of breasts are there?"

The old man thinks for a moment and replies, "As I recall, son, there are three. Yes, that's right. Three."

"Three, Grandpa?" says the kid. "How come just three?"

"Well," says the old man, "think of it this way. When a woman is in her 20s, her breasts are like melons—all nice and round and firm. Then when she's in her 30s and 40s, they become pear-shaped but are still nice to look at. When she's in her 50s, however, they start to look like onions."

"Onions?" says the boy.

"Yes, onions," says the old man. "You look at them and you want to cry."

An adolescent girl asks her grandmother, "Grandma, how many kinds of weenies are there?"

The old lady thinks for a moment and replies, "Well, as I recall, dear, there are three. Yes, that's right. Three."

"Three, Grandma?" says the kid. "How come just three?"

"Well," says the old woman, "think of it this way. When a young man is in his 20s, his weenie is like an oak, strong and hard. When he's in his 30s, 40s and even his 50s, his weenie is like a birch tree—flexible but still functional. When he's in his 60s and 70s, however, his weenie is like a Christmas tree."

"A Christmas tree?" says the girl.

"Yes, a Christmas tree," says the old woman. "All dried up with balls that are only there for decoration."

An Amish guy and his grandson visit a new suburban shopping mall for the first time.

They are amazed at everything they see: the bright lights, the busy stores and the colorful arrays of merchandise on display. But the one thing that fascinates the old man the most is the sight of a shiny new elevator. He stands and watches it intently, noting how people get on, the door closes and they seemingly disappear.

He is particularly intrigued when he sees as an old lady push her wheelchair up to the elevator. He sees the doors open, then close behind her. Then some small circles over the doors light up, and a few seconds later the doors open again, and out steps a beautiful young woman.

The old man stands watching this in disbelief. And then, with a big grin on his face, he nudges his grandson and says, "Go get your grandma."

TOP 10 SIGNS YOUR GRANDPARENTS ARE STILL SEXUALLY ACTIVE

10. You find your grandmother handcuffed to her walker.

9. You can hear their bedsprings squeaking—as well as their joints.

8. Your grandfather keeps rubbing his crotch and complaining about "denture burn."

7. Grandma starts baking Viagra-chip cookies.

6. Grandma often looks longingly at Grandpa's crotch and then claps her hands twice.

5. At night, your grandparents always put their teeth in the same glass.

4. When Grandma says she's going to take a nap, she always takes with her a hot water bottle, a blankie and a personal vibrator.

3. As Grandma leaves the room, Grandpa whistles, points at her ass and says, "Goddammit, that woman still looks good in polyester."

2. Down at the Senior's Club, Grandma wins first prize in a "wet shawl" contest.

1. Your grandparents' Ultramatic adjustable bed is always set for "Doggy-style."

A Boomer-aged woman decides that she can no longer look after her elderly mother, so she commits her to a nursing home for a trial period.

She drops her mother off one afternoon and promises to come back the next day to check on her.

The next morning, the nurses bathe the old lady, give her breakfast and sit her in a chair in front of a window overlooking the garden. After a while they notice that she has slumped over to one side of her chair, so a nurse rushes over and straightens her up. A few minutes later, the nurses notice that the old woman is tilting the other way, so another nurse dashes to her assistance and gets her sitting up straight again. This goes on all morning.

That afternoon, the daughter returns to see how her mother is settling in.

"How do you like it here?" she says. "Are they treating you well?"

"Oh fine," replies the old lady. "Except for some strange reason they won't let me fart!"

Young Geoffrey is thinking about asking his girlfriend to marry him, but he's nervous about taking the plunge so he asks his grandfather for some words of wisdom.

"Grandpa," he says, "you and Grandma have been married for over 40 years. Do you ever wish you'd stayed a single man?"

"Well, I'll tell ya, sonny," replies the grandfather. "Over the years I've learned that marriage is just about the best teacher of all. It teaches you loyalty, forbearance, meekness and forgiveness—and a great many other qualities you'll never need if you stay single."

Mavis is a 40-year-old woman who still lives at home with her parents. One morning her mother enters her room while she is playing with a new personal vibrator.

"What is this all about?" asks the mother.

"Oh, Mom, this is so embarrassing," says Mavis. "But I'm 40 years old, I don't have a boyfriend and I doubt if I'll ever get married. This vibrator will have to serve as my husband."

> "My doctor tells me I should start slowing down, but there are more old drunks than there are old doctors, so let's have another round."
>
> –Willie Nelson

The next day Mavis comes home early from work and discovers her mother sitting in the living room with a drink in one hand and the new vibrator buzzing away under her dress.

"Mother!" she says. "What are you doing?"

The mother replies, "I'm just having a drink with my new son-in-law."

An elderly couple is celebrating their golden wedding anniversary with friends and family in an upscale restaurant.

Their three sons, each of whom is a successful and independently wealthy businessman, show up late.

When the youngest son arrives, he says, "Sorry I'm late; I've had a helluva day, and I've been much too busy lately to go out and buy you a present."

The middle son arrives shortly after with a similar story: "Sorry I'm late, folks," he says, "but I've been at work all day, my Jaguar had a flat tire on my way here and there was no time to buy you a present."

The eldest son arrives last. "Sorry, Mom and Dad, I was busy closing a big deal this afternoon and couldn't get out to buy you a present," he says.

> "As you grow old, you lose your interest in sex, your friends drift away and your family ignores you. There are many other advantages, of course, but these would seem to me the outstanding ones."
>
> –Richard Needham

After a huge dinner, the father stands up and gives a speech. As he finishes, he turns to his sons and says, "There's something your mother and I have wanted to tell you three for a long time. As you know, we came to this country penniless. We worked hard and sent all of you to university so that you'd have a head start in your careers. Unfortunately, we were so busy back then that we never got around to getting married. We're sorry, but we thought it was time that you knew."

The three sons are shocked. One of them says, "So, you mean we're all bastards?"

"Yes," replies the father. "And goddamned cheap ones, too."

A naive young guy who has led a sheltered life in a rural community in Wyoming is about to get married. He knows very little about sex, and because his father died young, he decides to ask his aging grandfather for advice.

"How often should I expect to have sex after I'm married, Grandpa?" he asks.

"Well," replies the old man, "when you're first married, you'll probably want to have it all the time—maybe even several times a day. Then, when you've been married a while, it tapers off a bit to maybe once a week."

"Wow! Several times a day!" says the grandson. "That's fantastic. But how 'bout when you've been married for a few years?"

"Well, I'm afraid to tell you that it tapers off even more," says the old man. "After five or 10 years of marriage, you might be lucky to do it once a month."

"How 'bout now?" asks the grandson. "How often do you and Grandma have sex?"

"Oh, well," says the grandfather, "it's a long story. But let's just say that, now, your grandma and I just have occasional oral sex."

"What's that, Grandpa?" asks the young man.

"Well, for us, it generally goes like this: at bedtime, she goes into her bedroom and I go into mine. And then she yells out to me, 'F**k you!' And I holler back to her, 'F**k you, too!' That's about all there is to it."

A little kid goes up to his grandfather and says, "Grandpa, can you make the sound of a frog?"

"Well, I can certainly try," says the old man. "But why do you want me to imitate a frog sound?"

The kid replies, "'Cause Mom says that when you croak, we can all go to Disneyland."

A grandmother asks her doctor for a prescription for birth control pills. "I need them to help me sleep at night," she explains.

"How will birth control pills help you sleep?" asks the doctor.

"Oh, I don't take them," says the woman. "I slip them into my granddaughter's orange juice when she's not looking. Then I sleep much better each night."

A Greek family decides that their aging grandfather can no longer live with them. But when they look for a Greek nursing home for their old pappous, they find all of them are full, so they settle on moving the old man into a home that is run by Italians.

Weeks go by, and the old Greek man settles into his new surroundings. Then one day his young grandson, Dimitri, comes to visit him.

"How do you like it here, Pappous?" asks Dimitri.

"Oh, it's not bad," says the old man. "But I feel like a bit of an outsider; I don't really fit in."

"How do you mean?" asks Dimitri. "What's the problem?"

"Well," says the old man, "let me give you an example. See that old Italian guy over there? He was once a great concert pianist, and even though he hasn't played his piano in 35 years, they still respectfully all refer to him as 'Maestro.'"

The old man then points across the room and says, "Now, you see that other old guy over there? He was once a judge, and even though he hasn't sat on the bench in 30 years, everyone here still reverentially addresses him as 'Your Honor.'"

Looking around the room once more, the old man says, "See that old geezer in the corner? He was once a great surgeon, and even though he hasn't practiced medicine for 25 years, they all still call him 'Doctor.' ...And then there's me."

The old man looks down at his feet and says, "Even though I haven't had sex in 30 years, they all still call me the 'F**king Greek.'"

A woman carrying a baby goes into a doctor's examination room where the baby is scheduled for his first physical exam. The doctor begins by checking the baby's weight, and he quickly determines that the baby is drastically underweight for his age.

"Is he breastfed or bottle-fed?" asks the doctor.

"Breastfed," replies the woman.

"Okay," says the doctor, "please strip to the waist and let me examine your breasts."

He begins to pinch her nipples and then rubs both breasts up and down, around and sideways in a thorough and detailed examination.

"No wonder this baby is underweight," says the doctor. "You don't have any milk!"

"I know," says the woman. "I'm his grandmother. But, hey, thanks for the exam."

> "Another good thing about being poor is that when you are 70, your children will not have you declared legally insane in order to gain control of your estate."
>
> –Woody Allen

CHAPTER EIGHT

Driving Disasters

A cop stops an Boomer man who is swerving back and forth as he drives down the highway. The policeman tells the guy that he'll have to take a breathalyzer test.

"I can't do that," says the old man. "I'm asthmatic. I'll have a wheezing fit if I try to blow in that thing."

"Okay," says the cop, "I'm taking you down to headquarters for a blood alcohol test."

"I can't do that, either," says the man. "I'm anemic. I'll pass out if you take any of my blood."

"Okay," says the cop, "get out of the car and walk in a straight line."

"Sorry, can't help you there, either," says the guy.

"Why not?" asks the cop.

The old man looks the cop straight in the eye and says, "Because I'm drunk, you asshole!"

Bernice is 88 years old and still has her driver's license, even though she can barely see over the steering wheel of her car. She is out driving one day with her friend, Edith, sitting in the passenger seat, when suddenly, to Edith's horror, Bernice drives through a red light.

A few blocks later, they fly through a second red light, and then a third one.

Finally, Edith can't take it anymore, and as they are approaching another intersection, she screams, "Jesus Christ, Bernice! Don't you see you've driven through three red lights?"

"Huh?" replies Bernice. "Am I driving?"

YOU KNOW YOU'RE TOO OLD TO DRIVE WHEN...

- a cop pulls you over and is surprised to find that you are sober
- it takes you more than five minutes to get in or out of your car
- it scares you to drive at the speed limit
- you notice that you always keep your turn signals flashing, even when you don't have a clue where you're going
- you feel compelled to stop and read each and every road sign
- you use cruise control whenever your leg falls asleep
- you back into a parking spot and just keep moving until you hear something crunch
- you inquire at your car dealership to see if they can install a "magnifying windshield"
- parallel parking suddenly becomes a 20-minute workout
- you boast to your friends that in the past six months, you've only had four accidents worth reporting

Ralph and Dick are two aging Boomers who are having a beer in their local bar.

"I'm going to get married again," announces Ralph, proudly.

"Do I know your new bride?" asks Dick.

"Nope," says Ralph.

"Is she good looking?" asks Dick.

"Oh, not really," says Ralph.

"Is she a good cook?" asks Dick.

"No, she mostly just heats up stuff she buys frozen," says Ralph.

"Does she have a lot of money?" asks Dick.

"Nah, she's flat broke," replies Ralph.

"Is she good in bed?" asks Dick.

"I don't know," says Ralph. "We haven't done much lovin' yet."

"Ralph," says Dick, "we've been friends for years, so I've gotta ask, why the hell are you marrying this woman?"

"Oh, she's got one or two good points," replies Ralph. "For one thing, she can still drive."

A cop stops an older man driving down a highway in the wrong lane. He asks, "Have you got any ID?"

The old guy replies, "'Bout what?"

A couple in their 60s is driving down the highway when they hear a commercial on the radio for Ex-Lax. The commercial's slogan is, "Take Ex-Lax and you'll feel young again!"

"Let's stop and get some," says the guy as he wheels off the highway into a drugstore parking lot. He buys them each a large pack, and once back in the car, they both swallow several of the pills.

An hour or so later, as they continue down the highway, the old guy turns to his wife and says, "Do you feel any younger yet?"

"No," replies the wife, "I don't. Maybe we didn't take enough."

> "Yeah, I know some people are against drunk driving, and I call those people 'the cops.' But you know, sometimes you've got no choice—those kids have gotta get to school."
>
> –Dave Attell

So the old guy pulls the car over, and each of them takes several more Ex-Lax pills.

Another hour goes by, and the old guy says, "Do you feel any younger now?"

"No, I don't," says the old lady. "But I think I just did a really childish thing in my underpants."

Jerry is an old fart who is speeding down a four-lane highway when he gets a call from his wife on his cell phone.

His wife says, "I just heard on the news there's an old guy driving his car the wrong way down Highway 77. Please be careful."

Jerry replies, "One car? You've got to be kidding me. There's hundreds of 'em."

A cop sees an old lady driving down the highway while working away with her knitting needles. He pulls up beside her, winds down the window and yells, "Pull over!"

The old lady shouts back, "No, it's a scarf!"

Several old guys are sitting around the dinner table in their nursing home complaining about their ailments.

"My hands are so shaky that I can hardly hold my fork," says one old lady.

"My cataracts are so bad that I can't see to put my teeth in," says another.

"I can't turn my head 'cause I've got arthritis real bad in my neck," says one old guy.

"You think you've got problems," says another, "my pills make me so dizzy that I can hardly stand up, even with my cane."

"Oh well," adds another old lady, "life here isn't so bad. Thank God we live in Florida, where we're all still allowed to drive."

A cop is investigating a terrible head-on crash on a two-lane country road. He runs up to the old lady who was driving one of the cars. "What happened?" he asks.

"The other driver wouldn't let me have my half of the road," says the woman, over and over. "He just wouldn't let me have my half of the road."

Then the cop goes over to talk to the other driver, who is a much younger man. "That old lady says you wouldn't let her have her half of the road," says the cop.

The guy replies, "I'd have been happy to give her half of the road if she had just let me know which half she wanted."

> "I failed my driver's test. The guy asked me, 'What do you do when you come to a red light?' I said, 'I don't know... look around, listen to the radio.'"
>
> –Bill Braudis

A randy old widow is walking out to the parking lot of her local supermarket with a bag boy who is carrying her groceries. She leans over to the young man and slyly whispers, "I have an itchy pussy."

The bag boy glares at the old lady and says, "Well, ma'am, you'll have to point it out to me, 'cause I can't tell one Japanese car from another."

George goes out to his car one morning, gets in, panics and phones his wife on his cell phone. "Call the police, Ethel," he says. "Someone broke into my car and stole my stereo, my accelerator pedal, my brake pedal and my steering wheel."

Ethel runs outside, looks in his car and says, "You senile old fart, you're sitting in the back seat."

An elderly woman can't get her old car to start, so she calls a local mechanic to come over and take a look at it. The mechanic fiddles under the hood for a few minutes and eventually he gets the engine to turn over and spring to life.

"What's the problem?" asks the woman.

"Crap in the carburetor," says the mechanic.

The old woman frowns and says, "How often do I have to do that?"

An old married couple is driving along a highway when a cop pulls them over. "You were doing 70 miles per hour in a 50 zone," says the cop.

The husband replies, "I'm sorry, officer, but I was just poking along doing the speed limit, and I had to speed up for a second to pass a truck."

His wife leans over and interrupts, "You're lying. You've never driven under 70 since we left home."

"SHADDUP, damn you!" screams the husband.

"And I see you haven't got your seat belt buckled, sir," says the cop.

"I just undid it when you stopped me," says the man, "so I could get out my license for you."

> "Have you ever noticed that anybody driving slower than you is an idiot, and anyone going faster is a maniac?"
>
> –George Carlin

"Baloney!" says the wife. "You never buckle it up."

The husband turns to his wife and screams, "WILL YOU PLEASE JUST SHUT THE HELL UP AND LET ME HANDLE THIS!"

The cop turns to the wife and says, "Is he always this abrasive with you?"

"No, sir," replies the woman. "Only when he's drunk."

A cop pulls over an old lady who is poking along at 22 miles per hour on a six-lane highway. When he approaches the driver, he notices three other old ladies in the car who are each wide-eyed and white as ghosts.

The cop says, "Driving slower than the speed limit can be just as dangerous as speeding."

"I don't understand," says the woman. "I was doing exactly the speed limit of 22 miles per hour, so what's the problem?"

The cop says, "The number of this highway is 22; it's not the speed limit."

"Oh, thank you for pointing out my mistake," says the embarrassed old lady.

"But before I go," says the cop, "I have to ask, is everyone in this car okay? Your passengers seem awfully shaken."

"Oh, they'll be all right in a few minutes," says the driver. "We just got off Highway 135."

Gillian is making breakfast one morning when her husband suddenly rushes into the kitchen.

"Be careful," he says. "Be very CAREFUL! Put more butter on those eggs! Oh, my god! You're trying to fry too many pieces of bacon at once. TOO MANY! Turn them! TURN THEM NOW! More butter, dammit! Quick, get more butter! OH, MY GOD! They're all going to run together! Careful. CAREFUL! I said be CAREFUL! You NEVER listen to me when you're cooking! Never! Hurry up! Are you crazy? Have you lost your mind? Don't forget to put salt on the eggs. You know you always forget to salt them. Use the salt. USE THE SALT NOW! C'MON, DAMMIT! MORE SALT!"

Gillian stares at her husband in disbelief and says, "What the hell is wrong with you? You think I don't know how to fry some bacon and eggs?"

The husband replies, "I just wanted to show you what it feels like when I'm driving the car."

Three widows are sitting around in their nursing home talking about their long-deceased husbands. One says, "Oh, my Bert was quite a man. Back in the day, he was some great lover, too. He was like a Rolls Royce in bed—smooth and sophisticated."

The second old lady says, "Yes, I know what you mean. My Leon was a great lover, too. Hc was like a Porsche—fast and powerful."

The third woman listens to all this and adds, "You girls had all the luck. My Wilbur was like an old Chevy—he needed a hand to get started, and I had to jump on while he was still going."

> "Life should not be a journey to the grave with the intention of arriving safely in a pretty and well-preserved body, but rather to skid in broadside in a cloud of smoke, thoroughly used up, totally worn out, and loudly proclaiming, 'Wow! What a ride!'"
>
> –Hunter S. Thompson

≼ CHAPTER NINE ≽
Diseases and Losses

A man in his 60s is lying in a hospital bed, hooked up with IV tubes and monitors. He is breathing with the aid of an oxygen mask. An old lady pushing a coffee wagon enters his room and asks him if he would like anything.

"Yes," says the patient, speaking with difficulty through the oxygen mask. "I wonder, could you tell me if my testicles are black?"

"I'm sorry," says the woman, "I'm not part of the medical staff. I can't help you with that."

"Oh, please, have a look for me," pleads the man, getting agitated. "I'm really worried. Please just tell me, are my testicles black?"

The old lady feels sorry for the guy, who is obviously in severe distress, so she closes the door to his room and says, "Okay, I'll have a look for you."

She pulls back the bedcovers, slides his hospital gown up, gently lifts his penis to one side and examines the man's balls. "No," she says, "they're not black. They look completely normal to me."

The patient becomes even more agitated and pulls off his oxygen mask and shouts, "WHAT I SAID WAS, ARE MY TEST RESULTS BACK?"

A man goes to the doctor complaining that he has lost his hearing in one ear.

The doctor looks in his ear and says, "Here's the problem—you've got a suppository stuck in your ear."

"That's great news!" replies the guy. "Now I know where I put my hearing aid."

Q: Why is the change of life called "menopause"?

A: Because every time a menopausal woman hears a man speak, she must pause...or clobber him.

An 65-year-old man goes to the doctor for a checkup. After the doctor examines him, he asks the old guy about his sex life.

"I can't complain," he replies. "In fact, I think I'm doing great for my age. I got married last year to a beautiful 29-year-old woman, and now she's pregnant with my child. What do you think of that?"

The doctor says, "Let me tell you a story. A friend of mine is an avid hunter. But he's getting up there in years, and he gets confused a lot. Anyway, one morning as he was heading out to the woods, he accidentally picks up his umbrella instead of his rifle. As he is walking along, he spots a deer, so he grabs his umbrella, points it at the deer, squeezes the handle and BANG! The deer drops dead."

"That's impossible," says the man. "Someone else must have shot the deer."

The doctor looks at the old guy and says, "Exactly."

A man in his 70s suffers a severe heart attack and is rushed to a Los Angeles hospital for open heart bypass surgery. He awakens to find himself in the care of nuns in a Catholic hospital.

After the surgery, a nun enters his room and asks him how he's going to pay for his operation and his hospital care. "Do you have any health insurance?" she asks.

"No, I don't," replies the guy.

"Do you have any money in the bank?" asks the nun.

"Nope, I'm flat broke," says the patient.

> "Health is merely the slowest possible rate at which you can die."
>
> –Martin Fischer

"Do you have any relatives who could help you?" asks the nun.

"I only have a spinster sister who, by the way, happens to be a nun," says the guy.

"Nuns are not spinsters," says the nun. "Nuns are married to God."

"Great!" replies the patient. "Then just send the bill to my brother-in-law."

A severely constipated man is sitting in a toilet stall in a public washroom. He's grunting and groaning and pushing as hard as he can, but to no avail.

Suddenly, he hears footsteps—someone walking, then running into the stall next to him. The runner slams the door shut and loudly relieves himself.

The constipated guy says, "I'd give 100 dollars if I could do what you just did."

"No, you wouldn't," replies the other guy. "I didn't get my pants down in time."

Q: What is 20 feet long and stinks of urine?

A: The conga line in a nursing home.

William and Sam are having coffee. William says, "I just got a new hearing aid that cost me $4000."

"Really?" says Sam. "What kind is it?"

William replies, "Twelve-thirty."

A 60-year-old guy goes to his doctor for a physical. Two days later, the doctor sees the man walking down the street with a gorgeous young woman on his arm.

"Just doin' what you told me," says the old man. "'Get a hot Momma and be cheerful.' That's what you said."

"No," replies the doctor, "what I said was, 'You've got a heart murmur, so be careful.'"

An older Boomer guy is in a drugstore shopping for adult diapers. He says to a clerk, "Do you have any brand other than Depends?"

"No, we don't," replies the clerk. "What's wrong with Depends?"

"Nothing," says the old guy. "It's just the name I don't like. To me, 'Depends' sounds kinda iffy. Do you have an adult diaper called, 'For Sure,' or maybe 'For Certain'?"

A middle-aged man goes to the doctor for a prostate exam. The nurse tells him to wait in an examination room and that the doctor will be with him in a few minutes.

The guy sits down in the room alone and notices three items on the doctor's table: a tube of K-Y Jelly, a rubber glove and a bottle of beer.

When the doctor enters the room, the guy says, "I gotta ask, doc…the K-Y Jelly and the rubber glove I get, but what's the beer for?"

The doctor looks at the items on the table, opens the door and yells out to his nurse, "I told you I'll need a butt light, a BUTT LIGHT!"

Q: Why do older women prefer to visit elderly gynecologists?

A: They like their shaky hands.

A woman telephones the nurses' station at a hospital. "Is it possible for me to speak to someone who can tell me how a patient is doing?" she asks.

"Why, yes," says the nurse, "I can help you with that. What is the patient's name and room number?"

"Sarah Sleeman in room 409," says the woman on the phone.

"Well, let me check," says the nurse. "Oh, yes, I see we have some good news. Her records show that her blood work came back fine, and all of her other tests look normal. Her doctor says she can probably go home on Tuesday."

> "Health nuts are going to feel stupid someday, lying in hospitals dying of nothing."
>
> —Redd Foxx

"Thank you," says the woman on the phone, "that's good news. You've been very helpful."

"Are you Sarah's daughter?" asks the nurse.

"No, I'm Sarah Sleeman in room 409," says the woman. "No one around here tells me anything."

Old Harold's hearing is getting worse, so his doctor fits him with a new state-of-the-art hearing aid.

Several months later, Harold goes back for a checkup. The doctor does a few tests and informs him that his hearing is now perfect. "I'll bet your family is pleased that you can now hear everything they're saying," says the doctor.

"Oh, I haven't told them I got a new hearing aid," says Harold. "No siree, I just sit there quietly now and listen to their conversations. I've changed my will three times in the last couple of months."

A menopausal woman goes to her doctor after having a series of hormone injections. "I'm having some terrible side effects from the testosterone injections you gave me," she says. "I've started to grow hair in places that I've never grown hair before."

"A little hair growth is a perfectly normal side effect after testosterone injections," says the doctor. "Where has the hair appeared?"

The woman replies, "On my testicles."

THINGS AN OLD BOOMER NEVER WANTS TO HEAR DURING SURGERY

- "Remember, save everything we take out. We might need all this stuff for the autopsy."
- "Dammit! Has anyone survived a 200 mL dose of this drug before?"
- "Looks like we're entering uncharted territory here, guys. This is gonna be a learning experience for all of us."
- "Oops! This patient already has some kids, right?"
- "I sure wish I had remembered my glasses this morning."
- "Wow! That's so cool. Now see if you can make his other leg twitch."
- "Accept this sacrifice, O Great Lord of Darkness."
- "Anybody know if this guy signed an organ donor card?"
- "What do you mean you want a divorce?"
- "Wait a minute. I'm getting all confused. If that's his liver, then what the hell is this thing?"
- "You know, I hear you can get big bucks for kidneys these days, and look here, this guy has still got two of 'em."
- "So let me get this straight: now you're telling me that we should have been operating on his right leg?"
- "Goddammit! Page 76 of this manual is missing."
- "Hey, you come back here with that. Bad dog!"
- "Hand me that shiny pointy thing over there, will ya?"
- "Huh? You mean he wasn't in for a sex change?"

- "Sterile? Of course it's still sterile. This floor looks pretty clean to me."
- "Stop! My contact lens just popped out."
- "Come on, guys, can we hurry this up a bit? I have a three o'clock tee time."
- "Hey, Ernie, unzip the bag on that guy in the corner. I think he's still moving."
- "What? Did I hear someone say this guy has no insurance?"

An old couple is sitting in a church pew. The woman leans over and says to her husband, "I just let out a silent fart; what should I do?"

The husband replies, "Get a new battery for your hearing aid."

Q: Why do old men fart more often than old women?

A: Old ladies don't shut up long enough to build up the necessary pressure.

Two guys are sitting in their retirement home talking about old age.

"I'm 93 years old and I ache from head to toe," says one.

"Oh, yeah?" says the other. "Well, I'm 97 years old, and I feel like a newborn baby."

"How so?" asks the first guy.

"I've got no hair and no teeth," he says, "and I think I just peed my pants."

A newspaper photographer hears that twin sisters who live in a local nursing home are about to turn 100, so he arranges to take a picture of them on their special birthday.

When he arrives at the nursing home, he discovers that one of the old ladies is almost totally deaf.

"Would you both please sit together on the sofa," he says to the woman who can still hear.

"WHAT DID HE SAY?" shouts the deaf one.

"HE WANTS US TO SIT TOGETHER ON THE SOFA!" replies the other sister.

"Now," says the photographer, "I must ask you to sit closer together."

"WHAT DID HE SAY?" yells the deaf sister.

"HE SAYS HE WANTS US TO SIT CLOSER!" says the other sister.

"Okay," says the photographer, "now please sit still for a moment while I focus."

"WHAT DID HE SAY?" shouts the deaf sister.

"HE SAYS HE'S GONNA FOCUS!" says the other one.

"OH, MY GOD!" shouts the deaf old lady. "BOTH OF US?"

A rural preacher takes pride in making his sermons relevant to modern issues. One Sunday he stands before his congregation and proclaims, "If you ever feel adrift in the sea of life, turn to the Bible for guidance. All life's experiences are immortalized in the good book, and it will help you to find your way to shore."

After the sermon, a Boomer woman walks up to the preacher and says, "I don't think every life experience is covered in the Bible. As a menopausal woman, I've looked through it for guidance on the unpleasantness I'm suffering, and I can't find anything to comfort me."

The preacher says he will study the matter and get back to her.

A week later, the preacher pulls the woman aside before his sermon and says, "I was right when I said every life experience is addressed in the Bible."

"Really?" says the woman. "Where does it mention menopause?"

The old preacher opens his Bible and points to a passage that reads, "And Mary rode Joseph's ass all the way to Bethlehem."

SIGNS THAT YOU MIGHT BE ENTERING MENOPAUSE

- You're convinced that everyone around you has an attitude problem.

- You know that everyone around you is scheming to drive you crazy.

- You notice that your husband suddenly seems to agree with almost everything you say.

- When you're having a hot flash, your husband jokes that there's no need to light the fireplace to heat the family room—he'll just sit close to you.

- The phenobarbital dose that wiped out the Heaven's Gate cult gives you about four hours of decent sleep.

- You need to put Post-it notes up all over the house to remember your children's names.

- Your husband walks in the door and cheerfully says, "Honey, I'm home," and you reply, "Well, if it isn't Ozzie f**king Nelson."

- You notice that you've started to take an interest in strange TV programs like Wrestlemania.

- You're convinced that your dryer has suddenly shrunk every pair of your jeans.

- You're so juiced up on estrogen that you decide it would be a good idea to take your Brownie troupe on a field trip to Chippendales.

- You're so dry that you go into your local Jiffy Lube and ask them to put you up on the hoist.

- You notice that you no longer have upper arms—your biceps have become wingspans, and some days you think you could take flight like a flying squirrel.

- You notice your husband admiring some knock-out young thing in a tube top and you totally lose it. You go up to her and scream, "YOU KNOW WHAT, HONEY? EVEN THE ROMAN EMPIRE FELL, AND ONE DAY THOSE BOOBS OF YOURS WILL, TOO!"

Q: Why did the proctologist use two fingers when he was examining an old guy's prostate?

A: He wanted a second opinion.

Three speakers are sitting together at the head table of a meeting of the Association of Hearing Impaired Persons. Since everyone in the audience is elderly or has difficulty hearing, the speakers give their presentations using sign language.

The first speaker begins his speech by rubbing his chest with both hands in a circular motion and then rubbing his crotch with an up and down motion. The other two speakers are mystified by his actions, and when he sits down after his speech, they ask him what the gestures meant.

"It's simple," says the first speaker. "The circular motion on my chest indicates boobs, or 'Ladies.' The crotch rubbing suggests 'Men.' So my speech began, 'Ladies and Gentlemen.'"

Not to be outdone, the second speaker stands up and begins his talk by placing his fingers above his forehead to look like antlers. He then proceeds to rub his chest and crotch, following the first guy's example. When he sits down, the other two ask him what the fingers on the forehead mean, and he explains that he was simply saying "Dear Ladies and Gentlemen."

The third speaker decides to go one better. When it's his turn at the podium, he, too, makes the antler symbol, the circular chest movement and the crotch rub, which is quickly followed by an obscene gesture with one hand.

When he sits down, the other two guys gang up on him. One of them asks, "We know what the first part meant, but what the hell was the rude gesture for at the end?"

The guy replies, "Isn't it obvious? I was saying, 'Dear Ladies and Gentlemen, it gives me great pleasure…'"

> "Waiters and waitresses become nicer and more caring. I used to pay my check and they'd say, 'Thank you.' That graduated to, 'Have a nice day.' That's now escalated into, 'You take care of yourself, now.' The other day I paid my check and the waiter said, 'Don't put off that mammogram.'"
>
> –Rita Rudner

A guy in his 60s suffers a massive heart attack and is rushed to a hospital emergency room.

After conducting many tests, the doctors inform him that he needs a heart transplant. They search for a suitable donor on the Internet and find that two hearts are available that would be compatible.

"One belonged to a social worker," the doctor tells the patient, "and the other came from a lawyer. Which one do you want?"

"I'll take the lawyer's," says the old guy, without hesitating.

"Don't you want to know more about the donors?" asks the doctor. "And why would you prefer a lawyer's heart over a social worker's?"

"It's a no-brainer," says the patient. "All social workers are bleeding hearts, right? And lawyers never use theirs, so I'll have the lawyer's, please."

Three old guys are sitting on a park bench. "Old age is a terrible thing," one guy says. "My hands now shake so bad that this morning when I was shaving, I cut my face to shreds."

The second guy says, "I know what you mean. The other day I was working in my garden and my hand was shaking so much that I accidentally cut the heads off all my flowers."

The third guy laughs and says, "That's nothing. My hands are so shaky that this morning I was standing at the toilet trying to take a pee and I came three times."

A Boomer guy is sitting in his doctor's waiting room. An annoying, nosey old guy he knows from his neighborhood enters the room and sits down beside him. "W-w-wa-what are you d-d-da-doing here?" says the guy.

"I'm waiting to see the doctor," says the Boomer.

"Wh-w-wha-why do you wa-wa-wa-want to see him?" says the guy.

"Well, if you must know, I'm here to see the doctor about my prostate problem."

"P-p-p-pr-prostate p-p-p-pr-problem?" says the guy, "Wh-wh-wha-what's that?"

"Well, if you really must know," says the guy, "I pee like you talk."

Ethel is a Boomer woman who can't stop farting. She goes to her doctor and explains to him that although she farts all the time, her farts are silent and have no odor.

"In fact," she says, "you may not believe this, but I haven't stopped farting since I arrived in your office."

The doctor gives Ethel a prescription and tells her to come back in one week.

When she returns, she tells the doctor that her problem is much worse.

"I'm still farting all the time," she says. "They're still silent, but now they smell terrible."

"Relax," says the doctor. "It may not be obvious to you, but I think we're making real progress."

"How so?" asks Ethel.

"Well, now that I've fixed your sense of smell," says the doctor, "I can start to work on your hearing."

Three old men are sitting in their rocking chairs in a nursing home. One of them says, "Man, I'd give 100 dollars to have a good pee."

The guy next to him says, "I'd pay twice that if I could just have a decent dump."

The third guy says, "Every morning at seven o'clock I pee like a racehorse, and by seven-thirty, regular as clockwork, I take a dump that a grizzly bear would be proud of."

> "People say that age is just a state of mind. I say it's more about the state of your body."
>
> –Geoffrey Parfitt

The other two guys nod admiringly.

"The problem is," he adds, "I seldom wake up before 10:00."

An old guy is being wheeled down the hall of a hospital on his way to an operating room. A nurse notices that the patient appears to be upset, so she asks him what's troubling him.

"I heard the head nurse say that it's a very simple operation," says the guy. "She said there's nothing to worry about and that she's certain it will all go smoothly. But I'm not so sure."

"Oh, she was just trying to comfort you," says the nurse. "What's so scary about that?"

The patient replies, "She was talking to my doctor."

Q: What are the three rules older men should follow to survive old age?

A: 1. Never pass an unoccupied bathroom.
2. Never waste a good erection.
3. Never trust a fart.

Question: How many menopausal women does it take to change a light bulb?

The menopausal woman's answer: One, ONLY ONE, DAMMIT! And do you know WHY? Because no one else in this GODDAMN HOUSE seems to know HOW TO CHANGE A LIGHT BULB! They don't even notice WHEN A GODDAMN LIGHT BULB HAS BURNED OUT! They'll sit in the dark for DAYS before they figure it out. And then they CAN'T FIND a replacement light bulb even though they've been kept in the SAME cabinet for the past 15 YEARS. And when, by some miracle, they DO find them, two days later, the chair they stood on to change the bulb will still be in the SAME SPOT! AND YOU KNOW WHAT? Underneath it will be THE WRAPPER THE GODDAMN LIGHT BULB CAME IN, because no one around here EVER PICKS UP OR TAKES OUT the GODDAMN GARBAGE. It's a wonder we haven't all been BURIED in the PILES OF GARBAGE in this house. It would take a GODDAMN ARMY to clean this place properly. AND DON'T EVEN GET ME STARTED ON WHO CHANGES THE TOILET ROLLS....I'm sorry, what was the question?

> "I'm getting old, but at least I can multi-task now. I piss when I sneeze."
>
> –Roseanne Barr

Betty, a 70-year-old woman, comes home from a visit to her doctor and says to her husband, "The doctor told me I have a pretty pussy."

"That's disgusting," says the husband. "How dare he say something rude like that to a lady in her senior years. I'm gonna phone that doctor and give him a piece of my mind."

After numerous calls, the guy eventually gets his wife's doctor on the line. "Why did you tell my wife she has a pretty pussy?" he asks. "It's disgusting, it's inappropriate, and it's unprofessional for a doctor to talk like that to a lady."

"I didn't tell her she had a pretty pussy," replies the doctor. "I told her she has acute angina!"

Marvin is sitting in his doctor's office. "I feel like hell, doc," he says. "My stomach is upset, I've got terrible diarrhea and I can't sleep at night."

"I can't find anything wrong with you. It must be the effects of drinking," replies the doctor.

Marvin says, "Why don't I come back when you're sober, then?"

Eileen goes to the doctor and tells him about her terrible constipation. "I haven't had a good dump for over two weeks," she says.

The doctor replies, "Have you done anything about it?"

"Yes," replies the old woman, "I go into the toilet for an hour in the morning and another hour in the afternoon."

"What I meant was," says the doctor, "do you take anything?"

"Oh, yeah," says Eileen, "I usually take a book."

An elderly woman phones her local drugstore and says, "This is an emergency. Do you sell Depends?"

"Yes, we do," says the pharmacist.

"And do you deliver?" asks the woman.

"Yes, we do," says the pharmacist. "Where are you ringing from?"

The woman replies, "From the waist down."

Three Boomer-aged men are talking over coffee one day.

One says, "I'm a once-a-night man, myself."

The second one says, "I'm a two-times-a-night guy."

The third one says, "My wife says I'm a five-times-a-night man. But she also says I shouldn't drink so much coffee before I go to bed."

> "Except for the occasional heart attack, I feel as young as I ever did."
>
> –Robert Benchley

Two elderly women meet at a Bingo hall.

One says, "Did you come on the bus?"

The other one says, "Yes, but I made it look like an asthma attack."

An elderly man goes into an ice cream parlor, limps up to a stool at the counter and grimaces in pain as he sits down. "I'd like a banana split," he says to the clerk.

"Would you like chocolate sauce on that, sir?" asks the clerk.

"Yes, please," says the guy, who is still cringing in pain as he settles into his seat.

"Some cherries?" asks the clerk.

"Yes, please," says the guy.

"Crushed nuts?" says the clerk.

"No," replies the old man, "arthritis."

Steve complains to his doctor that he thinks his wife is going deaf.

The doctor recommends that he try a simple hearing test. "Stand some distance away from her and ask her a question," he says. "If she doesn't answer, move closer and ask the question again. Keep repeating until she answers you, and then you'll know how hard of hearing she is."

> "You can live to be a hundred if you give up all the things that make you want to live to be a hundred."
>
> –Woody Allen

Steve goes home and calls out to his wife, "I'm home, honey. What's for dinner?" He doesn't hear her answer, so he goes into the room where she is sitting and says, "Honey, what's for dinner?"

Still not getting an answer, Steve walks up and stands a few feet away from her and says, "Honey, what's for dinner?"

Finally, she answers, "For the third time, I said we're having meatloaf."

Two old Jewish ladies, Sophie and Jody, are having a coffee. Sophie says, "My son met a new girl, and I'm hopeful that maybe he'll finally be getting married."

"That's good news," says Jody.

"Only problem is, my son says his new girlfriend has herpes," says Sophie. "What the hell is herpes?"

"I don't know," replies Jody, "but I have a medical encyclopedia at home, and I'll look it up for you and call you later."

That evening, Jody calls Sophie and says, "I have good news for you. There's nothing for you to worry about. I looked up herpes in my encyclopedia, and it says that it's a disease of the gentiles."

Two men are sitting on a park bench talking about their ailments.

One says, "I think arthritis is the cruelest disease."

"Nah," says the other guy, "I think cancer is much worse."

"No way," says the first man. "Think about it. With arthritis, every one of your joints gets stiff, except the one that counts most."

Alfie goes out to a bar one night and gets so drunk that he falls flat on his face on the floor. In his drunken stupor, he decides that what he needs is some fresh air. He tries to stand up, but he falls to the floor a second time, so he says to himself, "Screw it, I'll just crawl home."

The next morning, Alfie's wife finds him passed out on their doorstep. "You got so drunk last night that you had to crawl home, right?" she says.

"How did you know?" asks Alfie.

"You left your wheelchair at the bar again."

In the beginning, God created Heaven and Earth and populated the Earth with broccoli, cauliflower and spinach, green and yellow vegetables of all kinds so that Boomer Man and Boomer Woman could live long and healthy lives.

Then, using God's great gifts, Satan brought forth Big Macs. And then he led Boomer Man and Boomer Woman into further temptation when he adopted the phrase, "You want fries with that?"

And Boomer Man said, "Yes," and Boomer Woman said, "Yes, me too—and while you're at it, super-size them." They each gained 10 pounds.

And Satan smiled.

And God created healthy yogurt so that Boomer Woman might keep the figure that Boomer Man found so trim and fair. But Satan brought forth white flour from the wheat, and sugar from the cane, and then he combined them. And Boomer Woman jumped from size six to size 14.

So God said, "Try my fresh green salad." And Satan countered by presenting Boomer Man and Boomer Woman with ranch dressing, buttery croutons and garlic toast on the side. And both Boomer Man and Boomer Woman loosened their belts following the repast.

God then said, "I have sent you healthy vegetables, and vegetable oils and olive oils in which to cook them." And Satan brought forth so much deep-fried fish and fried chicken that they needed their own platter. And Boomer Man and Boomer Woman gained more weight and their cholesterol went through the roof.

God then created a light, fluffy white cake, named it "Angel Food Cake" and said, "It is good." Satan then created rich, dark chocolate cake and named it "Devil's Temptation."

God then brought forth running shoes so that Boomer Man and Boomer Woman might lose extra pounds. And Satan gave them cable TV with a remote control so Boomer Man and Boomer

Woman would not have to drag their enormous super-sized asses from their chairs and over to the TV to change the channels. And Boomer Man and Boomer Woman laughed and cried while watching the flickering blue light, and each gained more and more weight.

Then God brought forth the potato, naturally low in fat and full of nutrients. And Satan peeled off the healthy skin and sliced the starchy center into chips and deep fried them. And Boomer Man and Boomer Woman gained even more pounds.

God then produced lean meat so that Boomer Man and Boomer Woman might consume fewer calories and still satisfy their appetites. And Satan created Wendy's and its 99-cent double cheeseburger. Then Satan said, "You want onion rings with that?" And Boomer Man replied, "Yes!" And Boomer woman said, "Gimme a slice of pizza as well." And Satan said, "It is good." And Boomer Man and Boomer Woman finally went into cardiac arrest.

God then sighed and created quadruple bypass surgery.

Then Satan created government-run health care.

⋘ CHAPTER TEN ⋙
Assorted Eccentricities

An old guy sitting on a beach spots a beautiful young woman wearing a tiny bikini. He goes up to her and says, "If I give you $20, will you let me feel your breasts?"

The woman says, "Get lost, you dirty old man."

Undeterred, the old guy says, "I really want to fondle your boobs; how 'bout we up the ante to $100?"

"Look," says the young woman, "bugger off right now before I call the police."

"Okay," says the guy, "I'll give you $200."

"Dammit," says the woman, "what part of 'get lost' don't you understand?"

"Awe, c'mon," says the guy, "all I want to do is feel your boobs for a few minutes. How 'bout I give you $500?"

The young woman thinks about it for a moment and decides that $500 is a lot of money for getting felt up by a harmless old man. So she agrees, telling him, "I'll let you feel my breasts for $500, but only for a few seconds."

So she removes her bikini top. The old guy excitedly walks up to her and gently cups her boobs in his hands. Then, as he caresses them, he begins moaning over and over, "Oh, my God! Oh, my God!"

The woman is disturbed by this, and after a minute or two, she says, "Why do you keep saying 'Oh, my God?'"

The guy replies, "Oh, my God! Oh, my God! Wherever am I going to find $500?"

On a windy Sunday afternoon, a police officer notices a woman standing on a street corner holding onto her hat with both hands while her skirt is blowing up around her waist.

"The main obligation is to amuse yourself."

–S.J. Perelman

The cop says, "You know, madam, that while you're clinging to your hat, all these people passing by are looking at your private parts."

"Oh, I don't care about that," the old lady replies. "The way I see it, what they're looking at is 60 years old. But this hat is brand new!"

Mabel is the much-loved organist in her church. Never married, and now in her 80s, she is the most prim and proper woman in the congregation. One day, the pastor of her church drops by to visit her at home, and as he sits alone in Mabel's living room waiting for her to bring him a cup of tea, he's shocked to see that sitting on her old pump organ is a water-filled glass bowl with a condom floating in it.

When Mabel returns to the room, the pastor asks her about the strange object floating in the bowl.

"Oh, yes," says Mabel, "it's truly amazing how that works."

"Really?" says the pastor, who is thinking the old woman has a dark side that he wasn't aware of.

"You see," says Mabel, "I was walking down a street last fall when I found this little package on the ground. The directions on it said to put it on the organ and to keep it wet, and that it would prevent disease. And guess what? It works! I haven't had a cold all winter."

An older Boomer guy is walking down the street one afternoon when he hears a female voice say, "Please, sir, can you help me?"

He stops and looks around but there is no one there. He thinks he's imagining things. But then he hears the voice again: "Please, sir, I must ask you for a great favor."

He looks around. There's no one nearby. He thinks he's going nuts. Then he notices a little frog sitting in the grass. "Please," says the frog, "I beg you, please help me."

"What's your problem?" says the old guy.

"I was a beautiful 19-year-old princess," says the frog, "but then an evil witch put a spell on me and turned me into a frog. I urgently need your help."

"How can I help you?" asks the old guy.

"The only thing that will break the spell is to have a man kiss me on the mouth," says the frog. "Please do this for me so that I can return to being a beautiful, sexy princess."

"And all I have to do is kiss you?" asks the man.

"That's all," says the frog. "And as your reward, I promise I will make you feel young, too. I'll give you wild, passionate sex like you've never experienced before."

The old man picks up the frog and carefully places it in his pocket. "At my age," he thinks to himself, "I'd rather have a talking frog."

Q: What's the difference between a fat married woman and an old maid?

A: One is trying to diet, and the other is dying to try it.

A newspaper reporter is interviewing a woman who is about to turn 100 years old. "What is your secret for living such a long life?" he asks.

"The most important thing is to do everything in moderation," says the old lady. "I have always practiced moderation in my drinking and my eating habits, and that is why I have remained healthy to this day."

> "I'm at an age now when just putting my cigar in its holder is a thrill."
>
> –George Burns

"But I understand you have often been bedridden," says the reporter.

"You're damned right I have," replies the old lady. "Hundreds of times— but don't you dare put that in your newspaper."

An old guy is standing in line at the library with a stack of books about suicide.

The librarian sees the titles and says, "You can't take these books home. You'll have to read them in the library."

"How come?" asks the guy.

"You think I'm stupid?" replies the librarian. "You're not gonna bring 'em back."

Q: How do you get 100 old cows into a barn?

A: Put up a "BINGO" sign.

Two men are talking about their retirement and the ways they like to amuse themselves and make their days more interesting now that they have so much free time on their hands.

One of them says, "The other day, me and the missus were coming out of a store and we saw a cop writing a parking ticket. So I went up to him and said, 'Aw, c'mon, man, can't you give a senior citizen a break?' He ignored me and kept on writing the ticket. So my wife called him an ignorant son-of-a-bitch, and damned if he didn't start writing another ticket; this time for worn tires. Then I got real angry and called him a nasty fascist bastard and told him he should show more respect for senior citizens. He continued to ignore me and wrote yet another ticket. This went on for over 20 minutes. The more we abused him, the more tickets he wrote."

"So how much did it cost you in the end?" asks the other guy.

"I don't know," replies the old man. "Me and the missus went into town on the bus."

A retired guy sitting at home hears his doorbell ring and goes to the door to answer it but finds no one there. He looks down and sees a little snail sitting on his doorstep. He kicks the snail onto the lawn and slams the door.

Two years go by. One day, the guy hears the doorbell ring. He opens the door and sees the snail is back on his doorstep. The snail looks up and says, "What the hell was that all about?"

An old man gets on an elevator in a nursing home and stands beside an old lady.

"Can I smell your crotch?" asks the guy.

"NO, YOU MOST CERTAINLY CANNOT!" replies the woman.

"Oh, okay," says the old guy. "Then I guess it must be your feet."

A scruffy-looking old man, stinking of alcohol and stale cigarette smoke, walks into a bank, goes up to a teller and in a loud voice says, "I WANT TO OPEN A GODDAMN CHECKIN' ACCOUNT."

"I'm sorry," says the teller, "you can't use language like that in here."

"WHY THE HELL NOT?" says the dirty old guy.

"This is a respectable financial institution, sir," says the teller. "You just can't walk in here stinking of booze and talk to me like that and expect to be served."

"Look, don't give me none o' that shit," says the man. "I WANNA OPEN A GODDAMN CHECKIN'

ACCOUNT, AND I WANT TO OPEN IT RIGHT NOW!"

The bank manager hears the old man's shouting and comes out of his office to find out what is going on.

"Can I help you?" he asks.

"Christ almighty, yes!" says the old guy. "I JUST WON 22 MILLION DOLLARS IN THE LOTTERY AND I WANT TO OPEN A GODDAMN CHECKIN' ACCOUNT!"

"Hmmm," says the manager, "I think I see your problem, sir. You want to deposit 22 million dollars in my bank, and this stupid goddamn bitch is giving you a hard time!"

An older Boomer man goes into a drugstore every Monday morning to purchase condoms. The pharmacist notes that without fail, the man arrives in his store every Monday and always buys two dozen condoms.

One day the pharmacist's curiosity gets the better of him, so he says to the man, "My goodness, sir, you must have amazing stamina to go through so many condoms every week."

"Stamina?" says the man, with a laugh. "You've got to be kidding. At my age, sex is nothing but a distant memory."

"So what do you do with all these condoms you buy every week?" asks the pharmacist.

"Oh, they're for my dog," replies the man.

"Your dog needs condoms?" says the pharmacist.

"Yeah, that's right," says the old guy. "You see, I have terrible arthritis, and it's hard for me to pick up after him. So I feed him condoms and he poops right into little plastic bags."

An elderly gent goes into a Catholic church and takes a seat in one of the confessionals. "Forgive me, Father, for I have committed a terrible sin," he says to the priest.

"What did you do?" asks the priest.

"Well, here's the deal. I'm 82 years old, and I'm married with four children. I've got nine grand-children and four great grandchildren."

"So what did you do?" asks the priest.

"Last night I had sex with two 18-year-olds," says the old man.

"That's terrible," says the priest.

"Oh, but here's the best part," says the old man. "I did it twice with each of them. And each time was even more fantastic than the time before."

"Are you a practicing Catholic?" asks the priest. "When was the last time you went to confession?"

"Never," says the man. "I'm Jewish."

"So why are you telling me all this?" asks the priest.

"Father," replies the old guy, "I'm telling everybody."

A middle-aged guy is sitting on a bus. A teenager gets on the bus wearing brightly colored feathers in his hair that are dyed in stripes of red, blue, green and orange. The kid notices that the man is staring at him.

"What's your problem, mister?" asks the kid. "Haven't you ever done anything wild and crazy in your life?"

"Oh, yes, as a matter of fact I have," replies the man. "One time many years ago, I got really drunk at a party and had sex with a parrot. I was just thinking that maybe you're my kid."

Way out in the country at a old-fashioned general store, a pretty young clerk arrives at work every day wearing a miniskirt.

One day, a customer comes in and asks for a loaf of raisin bread. The raisin bread is kept on the top shelf, so the clerk gets out a stepladder to get it for him. As she reaches out while standing on the top rung, the young guy notices that he has a great view up her skirt and that she is not wearing any panties.

Word soon spreads throughout the community about the gorgeous young woman who wears tiny miniskirts to work in the general store. Before long, men from all over the county come in each day and ask for raisin bread. The young woman dutifully climbs the ladder to retrieve a loaf for each of them, and each of them takes a peek up her skirt.

> "Old age is always 15 years older than I am."
>
> –Bernard Baruch

One day, the young clerk begins to grow tired of climbing up and down the ladder to reach the raisin bread. While standing on the top rung, she spots an old man who is staring up at her. "Before I climb down," she says, "is yours raisin, too?"

"No," replies the old guy, "but it's sure startin' to twitch."

It's entertainment night at a seniors' center in Toronto. A hypnotist tells his audience that he is going to hypnotize everyone in the room at the same time. He takes out a very ornate-looking pocket watch and begins swinging it on its chain.

"Keep your eyes on the watch," he says. "This is a very special watch. You mustn't take your eyes off it. Back and forth, back and forth. Watch the watch...watch the watch...watch the watch," he says.

Hundreds of eyes follow the watch as it swings back and forth. But then suddenly it slips out of the hypnotist's fingers and smashes to pieces on the floor.

"SHIT!" the hypnotist yells.

It takes three days to clean up the mess on the floor of the seniors' center.

An old lady goes into a sex shop and says to the clerk, "G-g-good mo-mo-mo-morning! Ca-ca-can you he-he-help me?"

"I'll try," says the clerk. "What can I do for you?"

"D-d-d-do you se-se-sell vi-vi-vi-vibrators?" asks the old woman.

"Yes, we do," says the clerk.

"D-d-d-do you have th-th-the one ca-ca-ca-called ma-ma-ma-Magic Thruster?" she asks.

"Yes, we have that one," says the clerk. "It comes in small, medium and large, and in a variety of colors."

"Dah-da-da-does it vi-vi-vi-vibrate r-r-r-really, really fast?" asks the woman.

> "Nice to be here? At my age it's nice to be anywhere."
>
> –George Burns

"Yes," replies the clerk. "It has an adjustment, too. You can set it for slow speed, medium-speed or fast."

"Th-th-th-that's the one," says the woman.

"Would you like me to wrap one up for you?" asks the clerk.

"N-n-n-no," replies the old lady, "Th-th-th-that wo-wo-wo-won't b-b-b-be necessary. I ju-ju-ju-just ha-ha-have one qu-qu-qu-question ab-ba-ba-bout it. Ho-ho-how th-th-the h-h-he-hell do y-y-you t-t-t-turn it off?"

Q: How do you get 50 little old ladies to yell, "Aw shit!"?

A: Get another old lady to yell, "Bingo!"

A Boomer woman looks out her kitchen window one day and sees a strange little man standing in her backyard. She goes out her back door and says, "Excuse me, but what do you think you're doing in my backyard?"

"I'm a goblin," says the little man, "and since you caught me here, I owe you three wishes. Go on, make any three wishes you want."

The woman thinks for a moment and says, "Okay, I want a big new house, a BMW sports car and uh, two, no, make that three million dollars."

"No problem," says the little man, "but before I can make this happen, you must have sex with me."

The woman invites the little man in for dinner and drinks, after which they retire to her bedroom for a night of wild lovemaking.

The next morning, the little man wakes up in the woman's bed and turns to her and says, "I've got one question that I must ask you before I go. Tell me, how old are you?"

"I'm 56," says the woman.

"Jesus Christ!" says the little man. "You're 56 years old and you still believe in goblins?"

✎ CHAPTER ELEVEN ✎
Going Ga-ga

After administering numerous drugs to an aging patient who is showing early signs of senility, doctors at a gerontology clinic think his mental state has improved to a point that he may be able to live on his own once again.

But the head of the clinic, a cautious young therapist, decides that she will interview the guy herself and have the final say on whether or not he is fit to go home.

"Tell me," she says, "if we send you home, what do you think you'll do all day?"

"Well," says the man, "I was once a nuclear scientist, you know. So I've been thinking that I might pick up my research where I left off so many years ago."

"That sounds like an excellent idea," says the therapist.

"Or," says the man, "I might teach. There's so much to be said for sharing all the knowledge and technical know-how I gleaned over my long career."

"That would be very admirable," says the therapist.

"Alternatively," says the old man, "I may decide to write. There's a great deal of interest in the nuclear industries these days, and I'm convinced that I could play a valuable role in educating young people on how nuclear science will impact their lives."

"I couldn't agree more," says the therapist.

"And if all else fails," says the old man, "I can always just stay at home all day and continue my life as a tea pot."

An old man with Alzheimer's walks up to a woman in a bar and says, "Tell me, do I come here often?"

An elderly couple is sitting in their doctor's office.

"I have examined your wife," says the doctor. "And quite frankly, I can't decide whether she has Alzheimer's or AIDS."

"What should I do?" asks the husband.

"Here's an idea," says the doctor. "On your way home today, drop her off at the supermarket. Give her a list of groceries to pick up. Then, watch her carefully. If she gets lost, bring her in for more tests. But if she finds her way home and has the right groceries, whatever you do, don't have sex with her."

> "Your wrinkles show that you're nasty, cranky and senile, or that you're always smiling."
>
> –Carlos Santana

Three Boomer women are sitting around the kitchen table drinking coffee and discussing the problems of getting older. One says, "Sometimes I find myself standing in front of the fridge with a jar of mayonnaise in my hand, and I can't remember what to do with it."

Another says, "You think that's bad, the other day I found myself standing on the stairs, and I couldn't remember if I was going up or down."

The third one says, "I don't have any problems like that, knock on wood," as she raps her knuckles on the table. "Wait," she says, "that must be the door. I'll get it."

An old guy goes to the doctor for the results of some tests. The doctor says, "First, the bad news—you've got cancer. I doubt if you will live more than another year."

The patient sits quietly for a moment, taking in what the doctor has told him.

"Now for the good news," says the doctor. "You've also got Alzheimer's. Two months from now you won't remember anything I've told you today."

Edith is a Boomer-aged woman who is thinking about getting married for the second time. She is talking to her friend, Mildred, who is older than she is and going a little senile.

"I'm reading a book entitled *Sex and Marriage*," says Edith, "and all it talks about is the importance of mutual orgasm. You wouldn't believe it. According to this author, mutual orgasm is the key to a happy marriage. Tell me, when your husband was alive, did you two ever have mutual orgasm?"

Mildred thinks about it for a minute and replies, "No, I think we had State Farm."

The queen is touring a retirement home in England when she walks past an old man who is ignoring her and her entourage.

She goes up to the old man and says, "Do you know who I am?"

"No, I don't," says the old guy, "but if you ask the nice lady at the front desk, she'll be happy to tell you your name."

Q: What's a fun thing about Alzheimer's?

A: You get to sleep with a different woman every night.

Bertha and Wilbur are two old geezers who live in a trailer park in Florida. She is a widow, he is a widower. Both of their spouses have long passed away.

One evening at a community dinner, the two are sitting at the same table. As the evening progresses, they start to give each other admiring glances. Finally, after several glasses of wine, Wilbur gathers his courage, turns to Bertha and says, "Will you marry me?"

"Yes, I will!" replies Bertha.

> "First you forget names, then you forget faces. Next you forget to pull your zipper up, and finally, you forget to pull it down."
>
> –George Burns

Nothing more is said on the subject for the rest of the evening, and at the end of the dinner, the two return to their respective trailers.

The next morning, ol' Wilbur's memory of the previous night is a bit foggy. He remembers proposing to Bertha, but did she say "yes" or did she say "no"? He simply can't remember.

He eventually decides to telephone Bertha, and he explains to her that his memory isn't as good as it used to be. "When I asked if you would marry me, did you say 'yes' or 'no'?"

There is a long silence. Then Bertha says, "I answered 'yes, I will,' and I meant it with all my heart."

"That's good news," says Wilbur.

"By the way," says Bertha, "I'm really glad you called this morning because for the life of me, I couldn't remember who asked me."

Two retired professors are talking in the back garden of the retirement home where they live.

One says, "Have you read Marx?"

The other replies, "Yes, and I think it's these damn wicker chairs."

A nurse is making her rounds and checking on the patients in a nursing home. First, she enters Albert's room, where she finds him sitting up in bed with his arms held out in front of him, poised as though he's holding a steering wheel.

"What are you doing, Albert?" she asks.

"I'm driving down to Florida," Albert replies. "Yup, I'm in my ol' Chevy and I'm driving down to Florida."

The nurse leaves Albert's room and then enters George's room, next door. To her dismay, she finds him lying in his bed masturbating.

"Oh, George!" she says in mock horror. "What are you doing?"

George looks up and says, "I'm having sex with Albert's wife while he's away in Florida."

Q: What's the best thing about having a wife
with Alzheimer's?

A: You can give her the same gifts year after year.

Q: What's another fun thing about Alzheimer's?

A: You never have to watch reruns on TV.

A doctor is making his rounds in a nursing
home. He is asking each patient a few questions to
determine the severity of their dementia.

"What is your name?" he asks one old guy.

"Napoleon Bonaparte,"
replies the guy.

"How do you know
you're Napoleon?" asks the
doctor.

"God told me," says the
guy.

> "What a waste it is to
> lose one's mind. Or not
> to have a mind is being
> very wasteful."
>
> –Dan Quale

A patient sitting on the opposite side of the room
yells out, "Oh, no, I didn't!"

Two women are sitting in their wheelchairs in
a nursing home in Newfoundland. Out of the blue,
one of them says, "Tell me, do you remember the
minuet?"

The other old lady thinks for a moment and replies, "You know, I don't even remember the ones I slept with."

A minister notices that one of his parishioners, a frail, slightly senile woman, puts $1000 in the collection plate every Sunday. She is by far the most generous donor to his collection plate, so one Sunday as she is leaving, he stops her to thank her for her ongoing support.

"We really appreciate your generosity," he says.

"Oh, I'm happy to contribute," says the old lady. "My son sends me money every week, and whatever I don't need, I donate to the church."

"He must be very successful," says the minister. "What does he do?"

"He's a veterinarian," says the woman proudly.

"Where does he practice?" asks the minister.

"Oh, he has two locations," replies the old lady. "He has one cat house in Vegas, and another in Reno."

"Of all the things I've lost, I miss my mind the most."

–Mark Twain

Three residents in a nursing home stop a senile woman in the hall. One of the men asks, "Will you let us guess your age?"

"Sure," says the woman. "I'll bet you can't even come close."

"Okay," says one of the guys, "but first thing you've got to do is take off your blouse."

The old woman unbuttons her blouse and drapes it over her walker.

"Next, you have to take off your bra," says one of the other guys.

The old lady unhooks her bra and throws it on her walker.

"Great," says the third guy, "now take off your pants."

She removes her pants while the three men watch.

"YOU ARE 88 YEARS OLD!" the men all shout together.

"You're exactly right," says the old lady. "How did you know that?"

"It's easy," says one of the guys. "You told us yesterday."

A senile old guy named Winston is lying in his hospital bed calling out to his nurse. "Come quick," he says, "I have a terrible emergency."

The nurse rushes in and says, "What's the matter, sir?"

"This is terrible," says Winston. "I think my dick died last night."

The nurse thinks the old guy has really lost it this time, and she decides that the best thing to do is just to humor him. She lifts his hospital gown and pretends to examine his organ. "Oh, I'm sure it's okay, Winston," she says. "It looks fine to me. You have nothing to worry about."

Later that day, a doctor making his rounds drops by Winston's room. "How are you today, sir?" he asks.

"Oh, I'm okay," says Winston, "but my dick died last night."

The doctor makes a note that Winston's dementia is worsening, and he, too, decides that the best course of action is just to string the old guy along.

"I'm very sorry to hear that, Winston," he says. "You have my sincere condolences."

The next day, Winston is walking down the hospital corridor exposing himself to all the patients and nurses.

His doctor walks by and says, "Winston, why are you walking around with your penis hanging out of your pajamas?"

"I told you my dick died yesterday," replies Winston. "Today's the viewing."

George and Dave are two old farts having dinner with their wives one night at George's home. When the women leave the table and go into the kitchen, George turns to Dave and says, "Last night we went out to a fabulous new restaurant. The food was fantastic, and the service was excellent. I'd highly recommend it."

"Really?" says Dave. "What's the name of this new restaurant?"

George thinks for a moment, but his memory fails him. Then he says, "Help me here, Dave. What's the name of that flower that you give to someone you love? You know the one; it's usually red and it has thorns on the stem."

"You mean a rose," says Dave.

"That's the one!" says George. "Hey, Rose," he says, turning toward the kitchen, "what's the name of that restaurant we went to last night?"

Three old geezers go out for a walk.

One says, "Windy, isn't it?"

Another replies, "No, it's Thursday."

The third one says, "So am I, let's go for a drink."

An aging couple realizes that they are becoming increasingly forgetful. They decide that the best solution is to simply make a habit of writing down everything that they have to remember.

One night while they are watching television, the husband gets up to go to the kitchen.

"Would you bring me back a dish of ice cream?" asks the wife.

"No problem," replies the husband.

"Do you need to write that down?" she asks.

"No, I'll remember," says the guy.

"Okay," says the wife, "then I'd like chocolate ice cream with some whipped cream and a cherry on the top. Can you remember all that, or would you like me to write it down for you?"

"No, I'll remember," says the husband, who then leaves the room muttering to himself over and over, "chocolate ice cream, whipped cream, cherry on the top...chocolate ice cream, whipped cream, cherry on the top..."

Ten minutes later, he goes back into the room and hands his wife a plate of bacon and eggs.

"You senile old fart!" shouts the wife.

"What's the matter?" says the guy.

The wife replies, "You forgot my goddamned toast."

A doctor is giving three men in a nursing home a dementia test. He asks them, "What is three times three?"

Bill answers, "Thirty-nine!"

James thinks for a second or two and says, "Thursday!"

Ralph answers, "Nine!"

"That's excellent, Ralph," says the doctor. "Tell me, how did you get your answer?"

"It's easy," replies Ralph. "I just subtracted 39 from Thursday!"

After many years of playing cards together every weekend, several old ladies decide to break with their usual routine and go out to dinner together one night.

As they sit down in the restaurant, one woman turns to one of the others and says, "I know I've known you a long time, but for the life of me, I can't remember your name."

There is a silence that lasts for several seconds, and then the other old lady replies, "How soon do you need to know?"

A senile woman who lives in a nursing home flips out one day. She goes into her room, takes off all her clothes and ties a bed sheet around her neck like a cape. She then bursts out of her door into the corridor stark naked and yells, "SUPER PUSSY!"

She runs down the hall, stopping in front of everyone she meets to expose herself and yell, "SUPER PUSSY!"

Before the nurses can stop her, she goes up to an old guy sitting in his wheelchair, stands in front of him naked with her legs apart and again yells, "SUPER PUSSY!"

The old man looks up, stares at the grizzled old lady's body, and replies, "I think I'll have the soup!"

While walking into the lunch room of an old folks' home, a nurse catches a whiff of something unpleasant.

"Okay," she says, "who messed their pants?"

Dead silence. So the nurse walks back and forth around the tables until she finds the culprit, an old man sitting alone in the corner.

"Why didn't you fess up when I asked everyone who messed their pants?" she asks the old man.

"Oh," he replies, "because I'm not finished yet."

> "I am in the prime of my senility."
>
> —Joel Chandler Harris

Three Alzheimer's patients are standing on a platform in a train station. They are laughing and talking loudly and don't hear the whistle signaling the train's departure. Just as the train is about to pull out of the station, two of the men manage to jump on, leaving the third guy standing on the platform.

"Dammit," he says to the ticket taker, "I missed my train."

"Don't worry, sir," says the ticket taker. "There's another one leaving in 15 minutes."

"But you don't understand," replies the Alzheimer's patient. "Those other two guys were seeing me off."

Q: What's the best thing about Alzheimer's disease?

A: You can hide your own Easter eggs.

Ethel has a motorized scooter and is known around her retirement home as a bit of a speed demon. She is also quite senile. In her mind, her scooter is a high-powered sports car, and she spends her days roaring down the corridors, doing wheelies and seeing how fast she can take corners on two wheels. The residents in the home tolerate her, and a few even play along with her games.

One day as she is flying down the hall past Weird Willy's room, he puts out his hand and says, "Stop! Have you got a license to drive that thing?"

Ethel rummages in her handbag and pulls out a napkin and holds it up for Willy to see.

"Okay," says Willy, "you may proceed."

Then Ethel speeds down to the TV lounge where Mad Michael jumps out in front of her and says, "Stop! Do you have proof of insurance for this vehicle?"

Ethel rummages in her bag and pulls out another napkin and holds it up for Michael to inspect.

"Okay," says Michael, "carry on, ma'am."

Ethel then zooms past the shower room where Creepy Calvin suddenly steps out in front of her, stark naked and sporting an erection.

"Oh, no," says Ethel, "not the breathalyzer test again!"

On Veterans Day, CNN invites a slightly senile old fighter pilot to be interviewed live on TV to talk about his experiences in World War II.

"There I was, alone in my fighter plane flying over Germany," says the old pilot. "There were a bunch of fokkers flying over me, and another bunch of fokkers coming up from behind..."

The host of the show, concerned that the old man's language might upset his viewers, interrupts the old man and says, "Excuse me, sir, but for the benefit of our audience, perhaps I should explain that a 'Fokker,' spelled F-o-k-k-e-r, was a type of plane used by the Germans. Isn't that right, sir?"

"Oh, maybe," says the pilot. "But these fokkers were Messerschmitts!"

A doctor is examining one of his elderly patients in his office. He says, "How are you feeling today, Mr. Roberts?"

Mr. Roberts replies, "I feel great, except the strangest thing keeps happening to me. Every night when I get up to pee, I open the bathroom door and the light goes on automatically."

The doctor assumes that the old guy is getting a little senile, so later that day he calls the old man's son, Ralph, but the son's wife answers the phone. "I'm concerned about your father-in-law, Mrs. Roberts," he says. "He told me that when he gets up in the night to urinate and opens the bathroom door, the light comes on automatically, and I think he might—"

"Oh, no!" says Mrs. Roberts. "Hold on a minute, will you? HEY, RALPH, COME AND SPEAK TO THE DOCTOR," she yells. "YOUR FATHER'S PEEING IN THE REFRIGERATOR AGAIN!"

An old farmer is sitting on his front porch one morning when he sees one of his neighbor's kids walking by his house carrying a roll of chicken wire. "What are you going to do with that?" he asks the boy.

"I'm going down to the back 40 to catch some chickens," replies the kid.

"That ain't gonna work, sonny," says the farmer. "You can't catch chickens with chicken wire."

But late that evening, the farmer looks out and sees the young boy walking past his house, dragging the chicken wire, and lo and behold, he's got a string of chickens attached to it.

A few days later, the farmer is sitting on his front porch, and the same kid walks by carrying a large roll of duct tape. "What are you going to do with that?" he asks the boy.

"I'm goin' down to the pond to catch some ducks," says the kid.

"That ain't gonna work," says the farmer. "You can't catch ducks with duct tape."

But later that day, he sees the boy walking past his house with a row of ducks stuck to the duct tape.

The next morning, the old farmer is sitting on his porch when the same kid walks by carrying a bunch of tree branches. "What have you got there, sonny?"

"Pussy willows," replies the kid.

"Hold on a minute," says the old farmer. "I'll get my coat."

Q: How many Alzheimer's patients does it take to change a light bulb?

An Alzheimer's patient answers, "Huh? Oh, wait a minute, I know the answer to this, it's, uh, let me think now, it's uh, 'To get to the other side,' right?"

A senile old man has hemorrhoids, so his doctor gives him four suppositories and tells him to come back in a couple of days.

The old guy doesn't know what to do with the suppositories, so he melts them down and drinks them. A few days later, he goes back to the doctor and tells him that the pain has worsened.

The doctor gives him four more suppositories and tells him to come back in a couple of days. The guy takes them home and drinks them.

When the man reports back to the doctor that he's still in pain, the doctor says, "I've given you eight suppositories, what the hell are you doing with them?"

The guy replies, "What do you think I'm doing with 'em, doc, shoving 'em up my arse?"

A pastor finishes his sermon every Sunday morning by asking his parishioners if any of them would like to come forward and express their thanks for prayers answered.

One Sunday, a little old lady volunteers to come forward to tell her story. She stands at the podium and says, "I have good reason to thank the Lord for answering all my prayers over these past difficult weeks. As many of you know, my husband Artie was in a terrible automobile accident two months ago. He has been in awful pain because he broke a lot of bones, and during the accident his scrotum was crushed."

"My presence of mind is frequently absent."

–Rain Bojangles

Hearing this, all the men in the congregation grimace in unison and begin nervously crossing and uncrossing their legs.

"You can't imagine the pain poor Artie experienced," she continues. "At first, the doctors didn't think they could help him because his scrotum was so badly mangled."

The men in the congregation gasp in horror and continue to cringe while holding their crotches and fidgeting in their seats.

"We prayed and prayed again the day the surgeons decided to operate and try to piece together the crushed remnants of poor Artie's scrotum," she adds. "They later told us that they even had to wrap wires around it to hold it in place."

Now everyone in the church is squirming uncomfortably at the thought of the horrible surgery that their fellow parishioner had to undergo.

"But now I'm happy to announce that all our prayers were answered," says the woman. "Artie is home, and the doctors say his scrotum should recover completely. Thank you, Jesus!"

The men all let out a collective sigh of relief as the pastor again takes to the podium and asks if anyone else has anything they'd like to say.

An old guy rises from the front row and slowly makes his way to the podium. "Hi, I'm Artie," he says. "I'd just like to tell my wife that, for the thousandth time, the word is sternum. STERNUM!"

CHAPTER TWELVE

Last Laughs

Old Dave is lying on his deathbed in his upstairs bedroom. As he draws his last breaths, he senses the smell of freshly baked chocolate chip cookies wafting up from the kitchen.

Driven by the smell of his favorite treat, he musters the strength to get himself out of bed and crawls downstairs. With great difficulty he drags himself down the hall on his hands and knees to the kitchen, where he sees his wife baking the chocolate chip cookies. With his last ounce of energy, he gets up on his knees and reaches out for a cookie, whereupon his wife slaps him on the wrist and says, "Don't touch those; they're for the funeral."

Sally dies and goes to heaven. She asks St. Peter, "Could I get together again with my dearly departed husband?"

Saint Peter says, "What was his name?"

"Bill Smith," replies Sally.

"That's a very common name for Boomer-aged men," says St. Peter. "We've got thousands of Bill Smiths up here. But sometimes we can identify people by their last words. Do you remember what they were?"

"Yes, I can," replies Sally. "He said if I ever sleep with another man after he is gone, he'll turn in his grave."

"Well, that helps a lot," says St. Peter. "I'm guessing the guy you're looking for is the one we call 'Spinning Bill Smith.'"

Two elderly women who haven't seen each other in many years meet on the street one day. One says, "How's your husband?"

The other says, "Oh, Ted died last month. He went out to the garden to get a cabbage for dinner, had a heart attack and dropped dead right there in the cabbage patch."

"That's terrible," says the other woman. "So what did you do?"

The old lady gives her a puzzled look and says, "I opened a can of peas."

An aging drummer who once played in a '60s rock 'n' roll band dies. He wakes up in heaven and finds himself on a stage where several musical instruments are set up. A stage door opens and in walks Jimi Hendrix, followed by Jim Morrison, John Lennon, Brian Jones, Buddy Holly and Otis Redding. Each of them picks up an instrument and begins tuning up.

The old drummer cannot believe his eyes. All his favorite rock 'n' roll legends are assembled on one stage. He walks up to John Lennon and says, "Hey, man, I'm new here, and I think this is fantastic. I can't wait to play with you guys. Is this really what heaven is like?"

"Heaven?" says Lennon. "You think this is heaven?"

At that moment, Karen Carpenter walks in, takes a seat behind the drum kit and shouts out, "Right, guys, let's start off with 'Close to You,' okay? One, two, three, four..."

Hector finds out that he has cancer and only has six months to live. He is walking down the street with his son one day when he bumps into an old friend.

When the friend asks Hector how he is, Hector replies, "Not good. I've just found out that I have AIDS, and I only have six months to live."

After the friend departs, the son asks his father why he told one of his oldest friends that he has AIDS when he really has cancer.

"One simple reason," replies Hector. "When I'm gone, I don't want him chasing after your mother."

Mavis, an elderly Jewish woman, dies. After her funeral service, the pallbearers are carrying her casket down a corridor in the synagogue when they accidentally bump it into a wall. They hear a loud moaning sound coming from inside the casket, and when they open it, they discover that Mavis is still alive.

She lives another 10 years, and finally she dies, this time for real.

> "I don't want to achieve immortality through my work; I want to achieve immortality through not dying."
>
> –Woody Allen

At her second funeral, which is held in the same synagogue, the pallbearers are once again carrying her casket down the same corridor. When they reach the spot where the casket got bumped the first time, Mavis' husband stops the procession. He turns to the pallbearers and whispers, "From here on, I want you all to proceed very, very carefully. And whatever you do, be sure to watch out for that goddamned wall!"

Harry calls the local undertaker and tells him that he needs his services to bury his wife. The undertaker replies, "Didn't I bury your wife about a year ago?"

"Yes, you did," replies Harry, "but I got married again six months ago."

"Oh, I didn't know that," says the undertaker. "Belated congratulations."

An 80-year-old woman is so depressed over the death of her husband that she decides to commit suicide. She gets out his old World War II army pistol and decides she will shoot herself in the heart.

Not wanting to botch it and become a vegetable, she calls her doctor and asks him to tell her exactly where her heart is located.

"Your heart is just below your left breast," says the doctor.

That night, the old lady is admitted to hospital with a gunshot wound to her left knee.

Edna is lying on her deathbed in a hospital with her husband, Jim, at her side. She asks him to close the door so they can have some privacy.

"After I'm gone," says Edna, "I want you to know, Jim, that it's okay by me if you decide to remarry. I don't expect you to live the rest of your life alone."

"Oh, God, Edna," says Jim, "you know you'll always be the love of my life. No one could ever take your place in my heart."

"Yes, I do," replies Edna. "But I have to be practical now, and I know that sooner or later, you're going to meet someone new. So just promise me one thing."

"Anything you want, my dear," replies Jim tearfully.

"Promise me that you won't let her wear my mother's mink coat," pleads Edna. "It's a family treasure, and I couldn't bear the thought of someone else wearing it."

"Aw, no worries, pet," says Jim. "Rachel is much too tall and thin to wear that old thing—oh, SHIT!"

Larry dies and leaves his wife Myrtle $20,000, every penny he has to his name. After his funeral, Myrtle complains to a friend that she has no money left and is flat broke.

"I thought you told me that Larry left you $20,000," the friend says. "How did you blow all that?"

"Well," replies Myrtle, "the funeral cost $6000, and the wake afterward cost another $2000. The rest went for a memorial stone."

"Wow," says the friend, "you blew $12,000 on a memorial stone. How big is it?"

Myrtle replies, "Oh, about three carats."

A poor old farmer named Orville is lying on his deathbed. He beckons his wife, Sophie, to come to his side to talk to him as he desperately gasps his last breaths.

"You're an amazing woman, Sophie," says Orville. "You were there at my side through those early years when we had no money and almost lost the farm when we couldn't make our mortgage payments."

Sophie sobs.

"You were there for me through those terrible droughts when I lost all my crops," he adds.

Sophie sobs some more.

"You were there when I fell into the thresher and lost both of my legs," Orville adds. "And you were by my side again when the whole place almost got washed away in the flood back in '76."

Sophie starts sobbing uncontrollably.

"And now, here you are again by my side as I lie on my deathbed," says Orville.

Sophie bursts into tears.

"You know Sophie," says Orville, "I've been thinking..."

"Yes, my dear," sobs Sophie.

"I've been thinking about this a lot," gasps Orville, as he is about to expire. "Sophie, you're nothing but a goddamned jinx."

A Bible study group made up of middle-aged and older Boomers is discussing unforeseen death. "If we knew when we were going to die," says the group's leader, "we'd all do a better job preparing for it."

She then asks each member of the group to think about how they would change their lives if they found out they only had four weeks to live, and to make a presentation at their next meeting.

The following week, the group asks Minnie to start the discussion. "If I discovered that I only had four more weeks to live," she says, "I'd go out into the world and minister the Gospels to those poor souls who have yet to accept Jesus into their lives."

"That's very admirable," says the group leader.

Next up is a Boomer guy named Ken. He says, "I'd dedicate all my remaining time to serving my family, my church and my fellow man."

"Excellent, Ken," says the group leader.

The next speaker is Robert, who is another Boomer-aged guy. "If I knew I only had four weeks left to live," he says, "I'd spend them driving across North America with my mother-in-law in my old Ford Escort, and we'd stay in a Motel 6 each and every night along the way."

"Why would you do that?" asks the group leader.

"Because," says Robert, "they would be the longest four weeks of my life."

Chester dies and finds himself at the gates of heaven.

"Before you can meet God," St. Peter says, "I have to review all the things you did in your life so he can decide what to do with you. But you're a tough case. I notice that you've never done anything particularly good, nor have you done anything particularly bad. Can you tell me anything you've done in your life to help us make a decision about you?"

Chester thinks for a moment and says, "Yes, I can. Once when I was driving along a remote country road, I came upon a young woman who was being harassed by a group of bikers. I pulled over, got out of my car and went up to the leader, a big muscular guy with tattoos all over his body and a big ring through his nose. I pulled the ring out of his nose and told them all to piss off and to leave this poor, defenseless woman alone or they would have to deal with me."

"That's very impressive," says St. Peter. "When did this happen?"

Chester says, "Oh, about two minutes ago."

Harvey is sitting in his doctor's office anxiously awaiting his test results.

"I've got bad news," says the doctor. "Your test results indicate that you've only got about 24 hours left to live."

Shocked, Harvey phones his wife at work to tell her the bad news. "Rush home right now," he says. "I've got to make the best of the few hours I have left."

When Harvey's wife arrives home, he says, "Quick, let's go upstairs and have sex."

A few hours later, Harvey rolls over and says to his wife, "C'mon, let's do it again! I've only got eight hours left."

So once again they go at it, and both of them eventually fall asleep. At dawn, Harvey rolls over and taps his wife on the shoulder. "I've only got three hours left. Do you think we could—"

"You've got to be kidding me," says the wife.

"Aw, c'mon, honey," begs Harvey. "I'll be gone in—"

"Look, Harvey," replies his wife. "Enough is enough. I have to get up in the morning—you don't."

> "I was thinking about how people seem to read the Bible a whole lot more as they get older; then it dawned on me—they're cramming for their final exam."
>
> –George Carlin

A priest is administering last rites to a dying man. "Denounce the devil," he says to the man, "and let him know how little you think of his evilness."

The dying man says nothing.

"You must denounce the devil," continues the priest. "Banish any thoughts of the horrible, evil influences that he has had on your life."

The dying man still says nothing.

"Why do you refuse to denounce the devil and his evil?" the priest pleads as the man begins to fade away.

With his last breaths, the man gasps, "Until I know where I'm going, Father, I don't want to piss anyone off."

A greedy old lawyer is lying on his deathbed. He is thinking about his life—all the crooked deals he pulled off over the years, all the ambulances he chased. "It's just not fair," he says to himself. "All that work, all that scheming and conniving, and here I lie at age 62 with a terminal illness."

He summons his wife to his bedside and tells her that he has come up with a plan to take his money with him to the great beyond. "I want you to fill two pillowcases with cash," he says. "Only put in large bills. And then I want you to place them in the attic above my bed. This way, when I die, I can reach out and grab the bags of money on my way up to heaven."

Several weeks after the funeral, the lawyer's widow is up in the attic, where she notices that the

"At my age, flowers scare me."

–George Burns

two pillowcases she filled with money are still sitting untouched, right where she left them.

"The silly old fart," she mutters to herself, "he should have told me to put them in the basement."

An insensitive undertaker goes up to a grieving widow who is sitting beside her husband's coffin. "How old was your husband?" he asks.

"He just turned 98," replies the sobbing widow. "He was just three weeks older than me."

The undertaker replies, "Geez, it's hardly worth your while going home, is it?"

Sam is an aging Boomer who is obsessed with his health. One day he goes to his doctor for his annual physical exam, and when it's over, he asks the doctor to assess his overall physical condition.

"You're in fantastic health for a man of your age," says his doctor.

"Really?" says Sam. "So tell me then, doc, what do you think my chances are of living to 100?"

"Well, let me see," says the doctor. "Do you smoke?"

"No, I've never smoked in my life," says Sam.

"Do you drink alcohol?" asks the doctor.

"Never touch the stuff—ever," says Sam proudly.

"Do you eat any junk food?" asks the doctor. "I mean, do you ever eat hot dogs, pizza, ice cream, doughnuts or cheeseburgers?"

"Nope," says Sam, "I never eat any of that crap."

"Then how about steaks, pork chops or barbecued ribs?" asks the doctor.

"No way," replies Sam. "I'm a strict vegetarian. My body is a temple; I only eat fresh fruit, nuts, yogurt, whole-grain bread, tofu and organically-grown vegetables."

"Okay, then," says the doctor. "Do you ever engage in any risky sports; you know, like rock climbing, sky diving, motorcycling or scuba diving?"

"Oh no," says Sam, "I've never done any of those things."

"What about sex?" says the doctor. "Do you ever engage in any risky sexual behavior?"

"Oh, hell no," says Sam. "I've lived like a monk for the past 10 years."

"Okay," says the doctor. "I have just one more question. Why the hell does a fun guy like you care about living to 100?"

After placing flowers on the grave of his dearly departed mother, a man is walking back to his car when he notices a guy kneeling at a grave, sobbing and wailing.

"Why did you have to die? Why did you have to die?" repeats the guy.

The man goes up to the mourner and says, "I don't want to interfere with your grieving, but your outpouring of pain is extraordinary. Whom do you mourn so deeply? A parent? A child?"

The mourner looks up and says, "My wife's first husband."

Three old Boomer guys are in a terrible car accident, and all three of them die. When they arrive at the Pearly Gates, St. Peter says to them, "Before you can be admitted to heaven, each of you must answer a simple question. What can you tell me about Easter?"

The first guy looks puzzled and says, "Isn't that the holiday in the fall when everyone pigs out on turkey and watches football all day?"

"Wrong!" says St. Peter. The guy disappears in a cloud of smoke.

The second man says, "Isn't Easter that holiday in December when everyone gets lots of gifts, and people decorate dead trees?"

"Wrong!" says St. Peter. And the second man disappears in a cloud of smoke.

The third old guy is getting nervous after seeing what happened to the other two. So he thinks long and hard about his answer.

"So, what can you tell me about Easter?" asks St. Peter.

"Well," says the guy, "that's the holiday that occurs in spring. It begins on the day Jesus was hung on a cross and made to wear a crown of thorns. He dies, and they bury him in a cave and roll a huge rock over the entrance to seal it. On the third day, Jesus is supposed to rise from the dead. So they roll the stone away from the cave entrance, and if Jesus pops his head out, it means there will be six more weeks of winter."

A miserly old guy lying on his deathbed tells his wife that he wants to take all his money with him into the afterlife. "I want you to put all my money in a box and then place it inside my coffin with me," he says.

The wife promises to follow his instructions.

A few days later, the old man dies. After his funeral service, his wife dutifully goes up to his coffin and places a large box in it beside his remains. She then returns to her seat where her best friend turns to her and says, "Surely you didn't put all his money in that box. That would be a terrible waste."

> "There are worse things in life than death. Have you ever spent an evening with an insurance salesman?"
>
> –Woody Allen

"Well, as a matter of fact I did," says the wife. "I put all his money together and deposited it in my checking account. Then I wrote him a check for the whole amount and put it in that box. If he can cash it, he can have it!"

Six old guys are playing poker and drinking in the games room of their Florida condominium. The drunkest guy, Herbert, makes a stupid blunder and loses $500 in a single hand. Then he suddenly gets a sharp pain in his chest, keels over and drops dead in his chair.

The other men are shaken by the sudden death of their friend, and within minutes they start to discuss who will tell Herbert's widow the sad news. "Let's cut the cards," one guy says. "Whoever draws the lowest card will go and tell his wife what happened."

They cut the cards and ol' Ernie draws the two of clubs, so he becomes the designated bearer of the bad news. "I'll be real discrete," he promises, as he staggers toward the door.

"Geez, man, you're pretty drunk," one of his friends cautions. "So be careful what you say. Don't make a bad situation worse."

"Don't worry," says Ernie, "I'll be real respectful in handlin' this very delicate matter."

Ernie goes over to Herbert's apartment and knocks on the door. But when Herbert's widow opens the door, he can't think of anything appropriate to say.

"I'm, uh, here to tell you some, uh, bad news…" he says, drifting off. He mumbles on like this for a few moments then he blurts out, "Your husband just lost $500 in a poker game and he's afraid to come home and tell you."

"Oh, yeah?" says the old lady. "He lost how much?"

"Five hundred bucks," repeats Ernie.

"Then do me a favor, will ya?" says the wife. "Just tell him from me to drop dead, okay? You got that? Tell him I said he can just drop dead."

"OK," Ernie replies, "I'll tell him."

A recently widowed woman goes to a psychic to try to make contact with her deceased husband, Arthur. The psychic goes into a trance, and within a few minutes, she tells the woman that she has contacted her dead husband. She then instructs the woman to speak directly to him.

"Are you there, Arthur?" asks the old lady.

"Yeah, I'm here," comes Arthur's faint reply.

"What's it like on the other side?" asks the woman.

"It's not bad. Not bad at all," says Arthur. "I get up in the morning, eat, have sex, then I take a nap. At noon, I have lunch, have some more sex, then take another nap. Then, in the evening, I have a big meal, get laid again, then go to sleep. Every day the routine is pretty much the same."

"Well, knowing what a horny old bugger you were on Earth, I guess you must be in heaven," says the old woman.

"Heaven?" says Arthur. "Hell, no. I came back as a jack rabbit in Wyoming."

A 90-year-old man is meeting with his financial advisor.

The financial guy says, "I've found a new investment for you that's guaranteed to double your money in five years."

The old guy replies, "FIVE YEARS! Are you kidding me? At my age I don't even buy green bananas."

A woman goes into the office of her local newspaper in New York City and tells the clerk that her husband just died and she would like to place a notice in the obituary column.

The clerk tells her the fee is $1 per word, so the widow says, "Just put 'George Brown died.'"

Amused by the old woman's thrift, the clerk informs her that there is a seven-word minimum for all obituary notices.

So the woman thinks for a moment and then rewrites her notice: "George Brown died. 2005 Oldsmobile for sale."

A lawyer dies and goes to heaven. "There must be some mistake," he says to St. Peter. "I'm only 55 years old."

"Not according to our calculations," says St. Peter. "We figure that you're about 82."

"How did you get that?" asks the lawyer.

St. Peter says, "We added up your timesheets."

A woman goes into a funeral home to spend a few minutes with her deceased husband's remains prior to the family visitation.

When she sees him decked out in the coffin for the first time, she tells the funeral director that he has made a mistake. "You've got him dressed in someone else's brown suit," she says. "My husband's suit is the blue one that's on the deceased person in the next room."

The funeral director says he will correct the mistake immediately and asks her to step out of the room.

A few minutes later, the funeral director asks the woman to come back into the room.

She notices that her husband is wearing the blue suit. "How did you do that so fast?" she asks.

"It was easy," says the funeral director. "I just switched...heads."

An elderly woman goes to her lawyer to prepare a new will. "I have two special requests," she says. "First, I want to be cremated. And second, I want my ashes scattered around the entrance to my local Walmart."

"Walmart?" says the lawyer. "Why would you want your ashes scattered there?"

The old lady replies, "It's the only way I can be sure my daughters will visit me twice a week."

A reporter is interviewing a woman on the occasion of her 106th birthday. "What is the best thing about turning 106?" he asks.

The old lady replies, "No peer pressure."

A 92-year-old Dutch man goes to his priest for confession. "Forgive me, Father, for I committed a terrible sin back in my youth. It was dreadful what I did, and I'll never forgive myself for it as long as I live," the man tells the priest.

"What did you do?" asks the priest.

"Well, back in World War II, I lived in the Netherlands, and one day I heard a knock on my door," he says. "It was a pretty young Jewish woman who asked me to hide her from the Nazis. I took her in, and she exchanged sexual favors for free room and board. I feel so awful about what I've done."

"Well, those were difficult times," replies the priest. "You took an enormous risk, but I can assure you that God, in his infinite wisdom and mercy, will judge you favorably for the good deed you did."

"Oh, good," says the old man. "But just one other thing. Do I need to tell her that the war is over?"

An old farmer is so distraught at the death of his wife that he breaks down in tears at the funeral. His best friend tries to console him by telling him that time is a great healer.

"Eventually," the friend says, "you will get over your loss. Who knows, in a few months you might even meet someone new."

"In a few months?" says the widower. "What the hell am I going to do tonight?"

A mortician is working late one night preparing for the funeral of Oswald, a local character and one-time ladies man, who is to be buried the next day. As he dresses Oswald, he notices that the man has the biggest penis he has ever seen. It is so big that the mortician decides that it must be saved for posterity, so he slices it off, puts it in his briefcase and takes it home to show his wife.

> "I've got all the money I'll ever need—if I die by four o'clock."
>
> –Henny Youngman

"You won't believe what I've got in my briefcase," he says to his wife that night as he opens the case.

His wife looks at the enormous organ and screams in horror, "Oh, my God! Oswald is dead!"

A Jewish widow has her husband cremated and takes the ashes home with her. She empties the urn on the kitchen table and proceeds to talk to her departed husband as she runs her fingers through his cremains.

"Irving," she says, "remember how you promised me a condo on Miami Beach? Well, I want you to know that I bought one with your insurance money.

"And, Irving, remember how you promised me a BMW sports car? You should know that I finally bought myself one of those, too, with your insurance money," she adds, while pushing Irving's ashes together in one large pile.

> "Always go to other people's funerals; otherwise they won't come to yours."
>
> –Yogi Berra

"Oh, and, Irving, how about that mink coat you promised me but never got around to buying for me? Well, I bought a gorgeous full-length one with your insurance money. And you should know that I also bought a diamond ring, some new furniture, a plasma TV, and I've booked that trip to Europe that we planned but never actually got around to taking—all with your insurance money.

"Oh, yes, and one more thing, Irving. Remember that blow job I promised you but never gave you? Well, get ready, 'cause here it comes!"

A young woman goes to a psychic to try to contact her dearly departed grandmother. The psychic takes her money and then drifts off into a trance. Her eyelids start blinking fast, her voice begins to warble, and then her hands flutter around the young woman's head.

"Is that you, Grandma?" says the young woman. "Are you there?"

"Yes, it's me," comes the reply in a quivering voice. "It's your old granny. How are you, my dear?"

"I'm fine," says the young woman. "I'm really fine. But before we continue, I'd just like to ask you one question."

"Anything, my child," comes the reply. "Ask me anything."

The young woman says, "When did you learn to speak English?"

Ezra is lying on his deathbed. He turns to his wife of 50 years and says, "Tell me truthfully, Lizzie, in all our years together, were you ever unfaithful to me?"

"Well, Ezra," replies Lizzie, thinking back over the years, "as a matter of fact, I was. Uh, let me think now…. It was two, uh, no, make that three times to be exact—but there were good reasons for each of them."

"Reasons?" says Ezra. "What kind of reasons?"

"Remember that time when we almost lost our house because we couldn't pay the mortgage?" says Lizzie. "Well, I went to see our bank manager, and afterward, he extended our loan."

"Those were tough years," says Ezra. "I can forgive you for that."

"Then there was the time when our little son Willy needed an operation, and we didn't have any insurance," says Lizzie. "I went to see the surgeon, and a few days later, he did the surgery for free."

"Oh, I often wondered why he did that," says Ezra. "But you saved our son's life, so I can forgive you for that. So what was the third time?"

"Oh, yeah," replies Lizzie. "Remember the time you ran for president of your golf club? And you came home and told me you needed 22 more votes..."

A newspaper reporter is interviewing an 84-year-old woman who is getting married for the fourth time.

"Who is your new husband?" he asks the woman.

"Oh, he's a very nice man," replies the old lady. "He's a prominent funeral director in this city."

Then the reporter asks her about her previous husbands.

"When I was in my 20s, I married a banker," explains the woman. "Then in my 30s, I married a man who owned a circus. After he died, when I was in my 50s, I married a preacher, and now in my 80s I'm marrying a funeral director."

"That's amazing," says the reporter. "So tell me, why did you marry men from so many diverse professions?"

"Oh, that's easy," says the old lady. "I married one for the money, two for the show, three to get ready and four to go!"

A widow puts a death notice in the newspaper announcing that her husband died of gonorrhea.

At the funeral, her brother-in-law challenges her, saying, "Ol' Jack died of diarrhea—why did you put gonorrhea in the notice?"

"I did it out of respect," replies the widow. "I'd like him to be remembered as a great lover rather than the big shit that he was."

Three old guys are involved in a terrible car crash on their way home from a bar, and all three die instantly.

When they arrive at the gates of heaven, St. Peter asks them what they would like to hear friends and relatives say about them when they gather around their caskets.

The first guy says, "I would like them to say they'll remember me as a great musician, a community leader and a good father and husband."

The second one says, "I hope they'll say I was an honest businessman, a dedicated philanthropist and a great humanitarian who made a difference in the world."

The third guy says, "I'd like to hear them say, 'Look, he's moving!'"

In the beginning, God made a decision to create the cow. God says to the cow, "Your job is to spend your days in the field with a farmer and to suffer under the sun, have calves and produce milk to support him. In return, I will give you a life of 60 years."

The cow says, "Geez, you've got to be kidding, God. That's a tough life you want me to live for 60 years. Tell you what, let me have just 20 years, and I'll give you back the other 40."

And God agrees.

> "I intend to live forever. So far, so good."
>
> –Stephen Wright

Then God creates the monkey. He tells him, "Your job is to entertain man. Do monkey tricks and make 'em laugh. If you do that, I'll give you a lifespan of 20 years."

The monkey says, "I'm to do monkey tricks for 20 years? I don't think so. Give me 10 years, and I'll give you back the other 10."

And God agrees.

Next, God creates the dog. God says to him, "Your job is to sit all day by the door and bark to warn your master of people who come by. I will give you a life of 20 years."

The dog says, "Aw, c'mon, God. That's way too long to sit on a porch barking. The monkey gave you back 10 years, so I'll do the same."

And God agrees.

Then God creates man. God says, "Eat, sleep, play, have sex and enjoy yourself. I'll give you 20 years."

"Say what?" says man. "That's it? All I get is 20 years? You're joking, right? Tell you what, I'll take my 20, plus the 40 the cow gave back, the 10 the monkey gave back, and the 10 the dog gave back. That makes 80, okay?"

And God says, "You've got a deal!"

So, all of this explains why for the first 20 years of our lives we eat, sleep, play, have sex, enjoy ourselves and do nothing. For the next 40 years we slave in the sun to support our families. Then for the next 10 years we do monkey tricks to entertain our grandchildren. And finally, for the last 10 years of our lives, what do we do? We sit on the front porch and bark.

Glen Warner

After toiling in the advertising and publishing industries for several years, Glen Warner dropped out of the rat race in 1978 and embarked on a career as a freelance writer. Since then he has earned his living as an advertising copywriter, journalist, author, biographer and award-winning travel writer. His articles have appeared in numerous Canadian, American and European newspapers and magazines. He is the author of *The Great Canadian Joke Book* and several books on contemporary art and artists.

Glen has always loved to hear and tell jokes. "I especially like the short ones," he says, "because of my increasingly limited attention span."

Glen lives in Toronto with his wife Diane and his faithful pal Zoey, a Shetland sheepdog.